HV
3006
.A4
L954

Lynch, Maureen.

Mary Fran and Mo

DATE			

MARY FRAN
AND MO

MAUREEN LYNCH

St. Martin's Press · New York

Library of Congress Cataloging in Publication Data

Lynch, Maureen.
  Mary Fran and Mo.

  1. Lynch, Mary Fran. 2. Mentally handicapped—
Biography. 3. Helping behavior. 4. Mentally handi-
capped—United States—Family relationships. I. Title.
HV3006.A4L954   362.3′092′6 [B]   79-16493
ISBN 0-312-51864-1

To My Family

ACKNOWLEDGEMENTS

Many thanks to our neighbors in Ballard and our friends in Seattle who helped us both so much during our year there. It's impossible to describe how much the Kiwanis Center meant to us; without it I don't think we could have stayed.

My deep appreciation to my friends who not only got dragged into our year but also into the book; and of course, Mark and Terry, who advised me to take up needlepoint, but continued to light candles for the book in all the churches they passed in Italy.

To my sister, Patricia, who patiently taught me the subway routes when I first moved to New York.

To ACRMD, especially everyone at my other home—Gercek Residence.

I'm grateful to many people at the New School for Social Research, especially Patrick Sheehan who let me take the year off before I had even started. And Hayes Jacobs who welcomed me back to class the second time, and was always available with advice and uplifting mottoes about writing.

Many thanks to Molly Woehrlin, a parent and a professional, who acted as my long-distance consultant. Many times I'd hang up the phone thinking I should have picked an easier one, but I never could have had a better one.

My mother, Matilda Lynch, filled in many of the gaps. Her support and advice were crucial to me, as they always have been.

Robert Bowers, Ignacy Goldberg, and Ann Tholfsen of Teachers College, Columbia University took the time to read my manuscript and were generous with their comments and support.

For never giving me suggestions, alterations, or ultimatums I have to thank Florence Amato, Bev Bauer, Olusegun Dairio, Jean and Richard Seltzer, Debbie Sillman, and Gil Suarez.

My talented, enthusiastic editor, Leslie Pockell, is responsible for making me finish the book just when I was beginning to consider needlepoint. Both he and his assistant, Paula Reedy, treated me just like family.

There are so many people who have shared their stories with me. I hope that if you recognize yourself you'll be glad that you helped share some of the concerns of the growing number of people who want more than neat labels. Many things have changed in the past twenty years: we have the legislation, we have some of the programs, and there is certainly no shortage of books. I just hope we can take what is happening now and make it work for us.

CHAPTER 1

We stood huddled together on the corner of the dark, rainy city street. Rain bounced off the bus stop sign and flowed past the gutter.

Relieved to see the bus finally coming, I pointed and said, "Look, here it comes."

"You come with me. Just this last time?"

I had expected her to say that and answered quickly, "We've been practicing for seven weeks. You can do it alone."

"Okay. But tell me again—what street do I get off on?"

"Seventy-first," I answered, "I'll ask the bus driver to remind you when he gets there." I bustled through the sentence with much more calmness than I was actually feeling.

Worrying at the bus driver's nonchalance as I repeated the street number to him, I saw the door snap closed and the bus splatter into the left lane. It turned and its back wheels sprayed out at me.

As I watched the bus disappear down the street, I systematically listed the numerous dangers I imagined she would face on the thirty-five-minute bus ride home. And I sympathized for all those mothers mocked in cartoons as over-protective.

But with my faded jeans, sneakers, and shoulder-length, curly hair I didn't look like a mother. I looked like the twenty-year-old college student that I was. The person on the bus was not my child. She was my sister. My older sister. She was born "brain damaged" . . . "mentally retarded" . . . "with a limitation." The list of terms to choose from seems even longer than the bus route.

But the terms are unimportant. The one thing that is important is the phrase that my sister, Mary Fran, had come to repeat frequently in recent years: "I'm capable!"

Mary Fran, at the age of twenty-two, was attempting to understand her life. What had been loving and supportive now seemed confining. She knew she was mentally retarded. But she needed to know that it didn't mean she would spend the rest of her life riding a school bus to her job of sanding wood in a sheltered workshop. And that it didn't mean a social life limited to monthly dances. Mary Fran didn't care that professionals talked about "diverse alternative living situations pending appropriate funding." She needed something then and there.

She was reaching out, desperately attempting to understand the type of life she was to lead. She was grasping at straws. Unfortunately, she was also grasping at furniture, threatening to break it. Arms flailing, she screamed her frustration while stamping out an accompaniment. As poignant as her search was, she was becoming impossible to live with.

Our mother's attempts to find help usually resulted in Mary Fran's anger being termed a psychiatric difficulty. This was followed by the suggestion that tranquilizers were necessary to "keep her calm until we know what's bothering her." It seemed obvious to us, her family, that it was her sheltered life that was "bothering" her. We wanted a new program, but our only offers were drugs that would make her satisfied with the old one. It made so much more sense to accept her anger, offer her the chance to try for more.

This new Mary Fran was so angry, so frightening. Mom and I talked about what she seemed to want. An individual tutor would be perfect, someone who would work with her on developing independent living skills. We let our minds wander as we talked about the ideal. It was too perfect to dismiss. "We'll live together, just Mary Fran and me," I told Mom. "And we'll make our own program." She seemed to smile in relief as if she had been hoping I would say that.

It was difficult to know where to begin. Mary Fran had never been on her own before. When I asked her if she wanted to share an apartment with me, she asked, "What about your school?" That was exactly what I had been concerned about. It was the end of the summer, and I had expected to be home for only another week before going on to a university I had recently transferred to. I told her I could probably arrange to take the year off from college. "Okay, Mo," she answered, "Just a year, right?"

Of course, working out the details wasn't easy. There were calls to our sister, Patricia, in New York who worked as a waitress while going to acting auditions. And to our brother, Philip, who lived in Seattle and worked in a psychiatric hospital. Usually our conversations were unfocused. While we talked like the mature adults we were supposed to be, we kept thinking—what does our sister think she's doing? This doesn't fit into my life. Frayed nerves were stepped on. And feelings we didn't want to admit existed were put into words. But eventually, we came to a decision.

Mary Fran and I would share an apartment for a year. Combining the money I would have spent for tuition with some money from our savings accounts, we came up with what we thought would be enough to live on. We hoped that before the year was up, we both would have found jobs. But we didn't really know what to expect. All we knew was that during our year we'd work on the independent living skills Mary Fran would need if she was ever going to live away from home: things like shopping for groceries, using a laundromat, and getting around by city buses.

Though I felt like Mary Fran's mother as I worried about her first bus ride alone, there were other times during the year when she played the mother role, gently helping me face things I didn't want to accept. And other times we were equals; neither one of us playing teacher or mother—we were just roommates, friends . . . sisters.

CHAPTER 2

Seattle seemed the perfect choice for our move. Philip lived there and had offered to help us get started. He told us about a recreational tutoring center for mentally retarded adults that was sponsored by the local Kiwanis Club. He had visited the center, and relayed the director's message that they'd be glad to help. But just as important were the things we planned to do on our own. And Seattle seemed just the right size for our project. Once we had our destination settled we began to look forward to the adventure we had gotten swept into. And as we packed, we tried to imagine what the year would be like.

Philip and his wife, Betty, would be waiting for us at the airport. I looked over at Mary Fran and saw that she was watching two girls in dungarees and sweat shirts make their way down the aisle of the plane. They were carrying a pet cage.

"Wonder what that is," I said to Mary Fran.

"Probably cat," she told me, smiling at the girls, who were

too busy maneuvering their cage and knapsacks through the aisle to notice her.

"You should have a cat wherever you live next year," I told her.

"I'm going to live with Mom," she said quickly, looking at me with alarm.

I remembered her insistence that we would both live in Seattle for just one year, and then return home to Michigan together. Maybe she thought we were scheming behind her back.

"I just meant that usually when people get to be our age it's hard for them to live at home," I said. "They want to do things their own way. So they start thinking about going away, living with a group, or one person, or by themselves. You know, Fran, that kind of stuff. And they decide if they want to live in a big city or a small town. They still go back home to visit–it's just something to think about."

"Yeah . . . maybe. Not now," she added quickly.

I mentioned Christina, a girl I had gone to college with, who had just graduated and was considering joining us.

"What does she look like?" Mary Fran asked.

"Oh, she's about 5′4″, you know, as tall as Mom," I answered. "And she's got blonde hair . . . it's real long and straight. And her eyes are green. And she's always starting some new craft project. I bet she'd love to see your crewel."

I began to wonder what it would be like if the three of us lived together. The idea of having a third person was very comforting. But I wondered if it wouldn't just cause more problems. I had told Christina that she would be just a roommate, with no other responsibilities. But I wondered if it could really be that simple.

"Christina and Ingrid sister, right?" Mary Fran asked, naming my college roommate. "Look alike?"

"They're both blonde. . . . No, other than that they really don't."

I wondered if Mary Fran and I looked alike. Or maybe we

looked like students returning to college, like the girls with the cat in front of us.

I would probably be picked out as the sloppy roommate. My long, curly hair was haphazardly pulled back in a ponytail, and I had on sneakers, faded jeans, and a T-shirt. Frequent purposeful blinks marked me as a new contact lens wearer. Otherwise, everything else was in predictable collegiate order: paperback novel, Minolta camera, and knapsack.

Mary Fran and I are both tall, around 5'8". In weight, I fluctuate between average and chunky. Mary Fran, on the other hand, is always slim. Her bedroom at home is decorated with the many ribbons she's won in Special Olympics. Her specialty is the 300-yard dash. She had on neatly-pressed, blue corduroy slacks and a plaid blouse. Her dark brown hair was still the same style that we three sisters all had when we were young—modified Prince Valiant. She has a sprinkling of freckles across her face. And her face can go from warm and animated to tense and aloof. But I had never seen her as tense as she had been the past few days.

Watching her out of the corner of my eye, I realized that we actually hadn't been togther that much since our younger years. It had probably been as early as kindergarten that we began to separate. My enrollment in regular school began the long series of clubs, and lessons, and parties that were available to me and not to her.

The pilot announced that we were circling Seattle. Mary Fran and I craned our heads near the window, checking out our new home. It wasn't what I had expected. Everyone had told us about the weather—it varied only in the amount of rain. Constantly gray and wet, they warned. But as we circled, I expected to hear Pete Seeger burst into "This Land Is Your Land." It didn't look like a city; it looked more like a postcard. The incredibly blue sky was fenced in by mountain ranges. And the many hills that the city is built on seemed to be dotted with more pine trees than buildings. Throughout it all was water, either a bay, or a lake, or a river.

We made our way through the connecting ramp to the

airport. I wondered what mood our brother and sister-in-law would be in. Philip loves Seattle. Betty hates it.

We saw them behind a group of people. And once in the car, Philip began his talk on Seattle. Besides loving the place, he loves to play tour guide.

"Mt. Rainier!" our brother shouted as he pointed out the car window with an air of proud ownership. I later learned that it was because Mt. Rainier is so seldom visible. The clouds that usually obscure it have caused many Seattlites to accept its existence solely on the word of others. When it does appear, normally sedate people pounce on complete strangers as they scream in delight, "Mt. Rainier!"

Betty attempted to give us her view by warning us that the sunny, 80-degree weather was atypical. Two weeks later, mid-September, it was still in the 80's, and the weather report stated that it was a record-breaking rainless streak. Betty told us that we had brought good luck. I certainly hoped so.

We finally found a house to rent, after a week-long search. It was a large old one, painted a mustardy yellow. I called Christina to find out if she was going to join us. I described the window seats, hardwood floors, and French doors. I told her we were half an hour from downtown, near three bus stops, and only a few blocks from Puget Sound. I was doing an all-out sales pitch. The $240-a-month rent seemed too good to pass up, so I had signed the lease. I was relieved to hear Christina say that she soon would be joining us.

It was still sunny and warm, and Mary Fran and I explored our new city. We took ferry rides, shopped at the outdoor market, and rode the monorail. We pawed our way through the thrift shops in search of furnishings for our new home. As we measured the living room in preparation for rug-hunting, checked the clock before leaving for a movie, or gathered the correct change before a bus ride, we were practicing important skills that Mary Fran would have to learn.

Notebooks and lessons signaled school to Mary Fran. And school had come to mean failure. She usually approached academic situations with a self-conscious dread. In Seattle she faced many of the same "school" concepts. But this time the skills were applied, and for the first time they seemed to make sense.

No matter how many times we rode the bus during the day, I would ask, "How much change do we need?" In the beginning I answered alone, "A nickel and a quarter." But soon Mary Fran was smugly beating me to the question by saying, "You have a nickel and a quarter? Have to have 'xact change, Mo!"

One afternoon, after a particularly hectic morning of errands, we returned home. Though we were very tired, we decided to shop for the much needed groceries; we had had our fill of peanut butter sandwiches. Our shopping resulted in four bags, and we staggered the two blocks to the bus stop.

"Mo, don't have a nickel!" Mary Fran confessed as she dug frantically around in her pocket.

Since the bus was already coming, we didn't have time to get change. So I put a quarter and a dime with her quarter. I promised I'd explain it later. She watched with concern as I gave the driver the three coins, and she seemed relieved when he accepted my payment.

The bags were valiantly holding together. But as we got off the bus, a quart of yogurt popped out of Mary Fran's bag and oozed onto the sidewalk. As if it were a planned revolt, four oranges jumped out of my bag. Another bag announced its support by belching out a loud rip as its bottom seam split.

"Oh, damn!" I said. "I didn't think we'd make it."

"Damn bags!" echoed Mary Fran.

I told her to wait with the spilled groceries while I took the two whole bags home.

"No! Don't wanna stay alone!" she whined.

"Jesus, Fran! I'm in no mood to be nurturing." I said and stalked off with the bags.

I quickly dropped the bags inside the door, then ran the two blocks back to the bus stop. But when I got there not only were there no groceries, there was no Mary Fran. To have her gone and groceries scattered about would have been a perfect mystery setting. But both were so neatly and completely missing that I looked up and down the street, thinking I was on the wrong block.

But I was at the right place; the bus stop sign and yogurt-stained sidewalk assured me of that. I circled the block, wondering if she had somehow taken the groceries home. But she hadn't. And I began to imagine her surrounded by taunting faces, sirens, and impatient policemen. It was useless to continue walking around the block with tears running down my face. But as I stood at the bus stop for the third time, I didn't know what else to do. So much for youthful enthusiasm, I scoffed at myself; this time you really got in over your head. And I began to wonder what perverse Helen Keller-Anne Sullivan fantasy I harbored that I had actually thought I could pull it off.

Looking up, I saw that a woman and three small children were watching me from their living room window. They stood there impassively, as if in front of a giant television screen. I wished it were one of those cliché-ridden T.V. shows. At least I'd know where to find her—in the pet shop humming absentmindedly to herself and stroking a hamster.

Then, suddenly, a pickup truck stopped next to the curb. In it was a young bearded man in a flannel shirt, two bags of groceries, and my sister. Mary Fran rolled down the window and the man called out.

"We were looking for you."

"Yeah, well . . . I was kind of wondering where you were, too," I said, all the time wondering who he was.

"My wife and the kids and I saw that your sister was in a bind," he explained motioning to the picture window that framed the woman and three kids. "So we brought her out some new bags. I was going to give her a lift home, but she couldn't remember the address of your new place."

I had no idea what to say. I just stood there in amazement. I wanted to hug the man for acting as if it were so simple, for responding to her as if she were just any new neighbor in trouble. But at the same time I wanted to shake them both.

They sat there so calmly, looking at me. I felt like shouting at him, "It's not that simple! She isn't like anyone else, she *is* different." I had imagined her panicking and running down the street trying to find our house.

But she hadn't. I certainly felt like running away, though. How was I ever going to learn when to be sheltering and when to be demanding? I had almost gone back to her instead of going home with the groceries. Her cry, "Don't wanna stay alone!" was too painfully reminiscent of the Sundays when, as a little girl, she would cry when we returned her to boarding school. But I had been tired, so I kept walking.

Actually, nothing was turning out as I had expected. I had great plans of her growing independence leading to all sorts of things—shopping alone, riding city buses . . . but the past three weeks she had barely left my side. Even when I only went upstairs to the bathroom she would follow. It was true that she wasn't acting out any more. But if she kept following me so closely I would soon be the one who was having tantrums. I knew that our year together was going to be a big change from my self-centered student life. But nothing had prepared me for this.

CHAPTER 3

We soon fell into a pattern that shaped our days. Mornings we worked together on various skills by acting them out. Practicing them at home first took some of the scariness out of them. We made up skits around activities like answering questions at a job interview, using the telephone, depositing a check in the bank, asking for change at a store, and riding a bus.

With skills like learning to get around by city buses, the most important thing was breaking them down into a more easily understood series of skills, making them less overpowering. Most people make their way around using city transit without a second thought. But it's really very involved; it means learning where the bus stop is, remembering how much the fare is, knowing where to put the money, finding out how to make the driver stop at your stop, and then maneuvering your way to your destination. These things are all made even more difficult if your reading skills are limited; the signs and directions are of little help–they just become one more thing to have to grapple with.

Afternoons gave us a chance to work on the everyday household activities like grocery shopping, cleaning, cooking, and using a laundromat.

Like all the things we did, these involved repetition. But unlike the repetition of a classroom, this repetition was born of necessity. Groceries ran out, so we had to shop. We got hungry, so we had to cook. After burnt chicken and raw steaks, Mary Fran soon learned the difference between the words "broil" and "bake." And so it continued; for her own comfort and survival she learned.

None of the things that we worked on were new to Mary Fran. But she had always followed, while others did them. Now it was becoming important for me to phase myself out, allowing her more independence until I wouldn't be needed at all. One of the first times we went to the laundromat, I made up a short errand so she would be alone for awhile. The next time I was gone longer, and reminded her to use dimes for the dryer. At first she was nervous alone, and was relieved when I returned. But gradually her confidence grew, and it was no longer important if I was with her.

One day we were practicing a job interview at home when Mary Fran wondered if she'd be asked if she was retarded.

"You might be," I told her. "What does it mean?"

"It's just something that happened when I was born," she told me impatiently, wanting to get on with the interview.

It wasn't the last time she was impatient with me. I was especially tiresome about trying to turn everything into a productive learning experience. I could be relied on to launch into a how-to lecture in the middle of the laundromat, while getting off the bus, or while making a grilled cheese sandwich. I remember her smiling face the first time she went across the street alone to the neighborhood grocery store. Now that I think about it, her expression—that I then saw as pride—was more likely relief that her little sister with the big mouth was staying home.

Though it made for a very intense situation for both of us, it was also exciting. Mary Fran took my demanding schedule as a vote of confidence in her. She appreciated the faith implicit in the challenge and gradually she began to trust herself more.

We had hoped to find some sort of on-the-job training program to help make her employable. The list of agencies that are supposed to offer such programs is extensive. The programs zig-zagged through my notebook in what was to become a familiar pattern. Each person I got in touch with offered little, but gave me two other people to call, who in turn gave me two more referrals. The reply was predictable: she was never quite right for their program, but "try this number." I felt as if I was caught in a game with rules I didn't understand, rules that somehow everyone else had been told, but were being kept from me.

At the end of the first month we had temporarily given up on finding a program, and began to look at the "Help Wanted" advertisements. One day I found a listing by a university professor who wanted someone for her two young children four afternoons a week. About to call the woman, I congratulated myself on our luck. We could take the job together, and it would introduce Mary Fran to some of the responsibilities of a regular job. And since the mother was a social work professor, she wouldn't have any prejudices against us; she might even have suggestions for us.

I called the woman, and she seemed interested when I listed my background in Head Start, tutoring, and camp programs. But when I told her our reason for being in Seattle, she quickly replied that it wouldn't be fair to put her kids "through that." "That," I surmised, was my sister and me. Before I could say anything she quickly told me that she didn't know anything about mental retardation, since her specialty was "death and dying." She just wanted a nice, normal college student, she explained. When I hung up, Mary Fran asked the result: "We go for a interview?"

"I guess we're out," I answered. "She wants someone closer to the university." Her face showed that she understood what

I was trying to hide. She reassured me, "We'll find something. Don't worry, Mo."

We had been right about Mary Fran's anger ending when she had more control over her life; but it was hard to predict her reaction to other things. It was as if she were weighing each new situation, trying to decide how much security to barter away for independence.

The hardest thing was just to stand alongside and watch. One Saturday morning we headed downtown for Mary Fran's haircut.

" 'Seattle Beauty College.' This is it, Fran," I said, reading the sign aloud. We walked in and were told to have a seat until her name was called.

"Mary Lynch," called a woman with a pink uniform and beehive hairdo.

"Me," answered Mary Fran.

"Okay, Hon." The woman smiled at Mary Fran. "What can we do you in for today?"

"Just a cut, kind of short."

Seeing the woman's confused look, I realized that my ears had once again automatically interpreted Mary Fran's speech. What the woman had heard was more like, "Dust a cut, tort."

After a pause, she sighed, "Okay, let's go."

Not knowing that we had come in together, she turned to me. I looked up from my magazine to see her give me a raised eyebrow look of exasperation.

"Why do I get all the weirdies?" she asked me.

I wanted to beat her up. Or at least say something that would make her feel guilty. But instead I watched Mary Fran walk calmly to the beautician's chair and sit down. When we left I wondered what Mary Fran would say if I tried to talk about it. Maybe someday we would. I pictured us in thirty years, getting together for a holiday. The incident is brought up and we talk about the early years, and how strange it is that people actually once thought like that. And together we would laugh about the woman with the lacquered hair and smirking face.

CHAPTER 4

Mocking laugher and pointed stares weren't new to me. Along with family trips and childhood friends, memories of my early years are full of jokes strangers made because of Mary Fran's difference. Our family handled it by developing the slick art of one-upmanship.

Some neighborhood children had once laughed at Mary Fran's ragged movements. "Lady, your kid's drooling!" They took up a chant at Mom on our walk around the block. At the time, I was only a year old and Mary Fran, three. But I remember the amazing sense of power as I repeated those same words some years later—words that had been absorbed into the family as a joke. "Lady, your kid's drooling!" I crowed expectantly. And true to my hopes, without really knowing why, it resulted in my family's shared laughter. It was as if by stealing our taunters' words we could take the power out of them; somehow show them as the senseless comments that they really were. I didn't understand it then. But I was soon to join in with complete understanding, attempting to take the sting out of overheard comments or purposeful jeers.

I remember my parents telling me when I was young that Mary Fran was mentally retarded. "All that means," they explained, "is that sometimes your sister will be slower." It wasn't something to joke or be embarrassed about. But neither was the special attention something to be patronizingly doled out. It was necessary, therefore it just *was*. The result of my parents' effective indoctrination is that when people ask me what it was like growing up with a mentally retarded sister, I have trouble answering. The reformer's zeal rises in me as I sense an opportunity to make a conversion, and I attempt to dredge up a gut-grabbing anecdote. But an answer doesn't come easily. I never thought of her as my "retarded sister."

Mary Fran's special needs, of course, affected our family—our attitudes, values, involvements. But it's difficult for me to dissect things neatly and understand the extent of her effect on our family life. I was born two years after Mary Fran, so I joined our family after it had become "different." In fact, I never knew we were different until people started telling me.

Maybe the two oldest children, Philip and Patricia, noticed the change. Philip was eight when Mary Fran was born, Patricia was four. The pictures in the family scrapbook, before Mary Fran and I were born, show a very different family from the one I know. My father, a tall, athletic man, was busy with his growing law practice. My mother, trained as a nurse, was involved with the many responsibilities of raising a family. In many of the pictures, Philip is riding a bicycle and wearing a sweater from our father's alma mater—Notre Dame. Many shots of Patricia show her in a leotard at dance lessons and recitals. The circle is completed by Lady, the family's Lassie look-alike pet collie. Two years after the later pictures were taken, the family would have two new members, an infant named Maureen, and two-year-old Mary Frances, whose slow development would cause our mother to draw on her nursing experience as she searched for a diagnosis.

The cause of Mary Fran's impairment isn't known. Mom cites a long and difficult labor, which could have resulted in a lack of sufficient oxygen for Mary Fran. Digging deeper, Mom remembers problems during the seventh month of pregnancy. She was busy one day, working on a church bazaar—carrying chairs, putting up decorations, and climbing stairs. That night, she hemorrhaged. But no other complications resulted, so the situation passed with little concern. It was 1951, and sophisticated tests weren't available. She had a checkup, and received a doctor's reassuring smile and pat on the shoulder.

The question of cause is a painful one. I ask it wondering how it is that Mary Fran is different. But to my parents it brings back the time when they could think of nothing but—why did it happen, what did I do wrong, when was it that I hurt our child?

Pediatricians diagnosed Mary Fran as hyperactive. But at that time there were few theories on hyperactivity. The only intervention was a prescription of dilantin for the mild seizures she had. Hyperactivity and seizures are typical signs of brain damage.

Brain damage doesn't always result in impaired intellectual potential. Some clinics diagnosed Mary Fran as mentally retarded, others said that she was definitely not, but that she did have a language dysfunction. Our family's story is one that many other families have experienced: conflicting diagnosis, referrals to limited or nonexistent programs, and recommendations that institutionalization would be "the best for all concerned."

But my parents did not agree that an institution would be the best place for Mary Fran. They wanted her to stay at home. But how could they help her, they reasoned, if they didn't know what was wrong? And so they searched for a diagnosis. Not necessarily one they wanted to hear. But at least the same opinion from two doctors.

Since we lived in a small town in Michigan, these trips to

doctors necessitated going to Chicago—a four-hour drive. I wasn't in school yet so I would sometimes go along. Other times I stayed at home with a baby-sitter.

When I was little I decided I wanted to be a psychologist. This may seem a strange career choice for a four-year-old, but in my young mind, the neurologists and psychologists and pediatricians that my parents took Mary Fran to all became psychologists. What wonderful people they must be, I thought, that my parents are always going to see them. How nice it would be if I were a psychologist and my parents would come to see me. Maybe I thought I could solve their problems, and end the series of doctors' appointments so we could all stay home together.

My parents decided that they were learning very little from all the diagnostic clinics. No one seemed to know what to suggest. When they did have a definite diagnosis, they were still unable to recommend a school program. The kind of special education programs that we have now didn't exist. The choice parents had then was mainly between large state institutions and expensive private schools. Few people felt that public schools should provide education for children with special needs. The attitude was largely: you *had* this different child, now it is your burden to take care of him.

Parents were then just beginning to organize into groups. But because the groups were new, and not well publicized, it would often be several years before new parents would hear of the others who had similar concerns. Chances were that, by this time, the parents had decided to put their child in an institution. The arguments had become too much to face alone. "There's nothing you can do" . . . "It's unfair to your other children" . . . "They're better off among their own kind."

For those parents who belonged to groups, education for their child developed into a cooperative situation. They would use a church basement, a recreational center, or each other's homes as classrooms. Transportation was often handled by the parents, taking turns driving a group of children to "school." If they were able to find someone willing to teach their children they would pool money to pay the salary. Otherwise the teaching would be done by parents, sometimes attracting retired school teachers or volunteers from the community.

My parents knew of no such group in our area. They felt the best thing for Mary Fran would be for her to grow up within her family and experience both the successes and failures that all children do.

One of the things that Mary Fran was not good at was getting dressed on time. That prompted the "just keep moving" philosophy. When she was young, she would dart from object to person and back again, seemingly too thrilled with everything to settle down with just one. At least that's the way I remember it. But Patricia, our older sister, remembers those years with a vividness etched into her mind because of the responsibilities she had. I remember the excitement of trying to keep up with Fran as she zipped along.

It didn't matter if we had been some place a hundred times or never before, every place was explored at the same frantic pace. Our basement, a new restaurant, or our grandmother's house amid the fragile antiques. It was always the same—zip to the wall, and then zip back to the center again to touch home base at our mother's lap, and before she could reach out with a hug we'd zip off to new territory. Maybe the restaurant's kitchen, oops—not supposed to go in there. No problem, just zip right out.

But if I remember those years with the satisfaction of an exhausted tourist who had a demanding tour guide, Patricia's memories are only of exhaustion. She remembers reaching for the blur of limbs as Fran rushed off a curb into the street. Or running after a speeding five-year old as she raced down the slick aisles of a department store.

Most of the chasing was done by our mother, though. She refused the pediatrician's prescription for medication. I don't know why; maybe it was a decision based on her nursing experience. Or maybe it was just the hope that it was just temporary, that the next day Mary Fran would wake up and no longer be hyperactive.

Mom had to develop the precision of a control tower navigator. Because, even though Fran had the speed of a tornado, she was also easily distracted. I remember a familiar phrase of our mother's was the frequently repeated admonition, "You kids act like you never get out!" But it was more than just the typical childhood search for adventure, as anyone who has ever lived with a hyperactive child knows. Everyday activities seem to take on a distorted importance. Just getting ready to go to the restaurant, the department store, or our grandmother's was a major project in itself.

But there was something about getting dressed that enabled Mary Fran to focus on one thing. And that thing was loose threads—first the loose threads on underpants, then the loose threads on a slip, then the loose threads on a dress. What a field day! After having ripped them all off and gathered them into a pile, she would then throw them away—which opened up another gold mine, exploring the wastepaper basket! She would throw away the threads sparingly, only a few at a time, savoring their descent into the wastepaper basket as if they were delicate snowflakes.

One morning when we were all bustling around getting dressed, Mom walked into the bedroom Mary Fran and I shared. Mary Fran sat on the floor in her underpants and anklets, delighting over the contents of the wastepaper basket. "Mary Frances!" Mom said in exasperation. Mary Fran quickly tossed the remaining pile of threads into the basket to get rid of the evidence. "Me hurrying!" she insisted. As Mary Fran had hoped, Mom's face softened as she said, "Oh, hon, you don't have to hurry." Lifting her to her feet, Mom directed her toward her dress that lay on the bed, and added with a laugh, "But just keep moving."

It was a difficult seesaw that our parents were on. They wanted their daughter to live as normal a life as possible. But they were often brought up short, wondering if they were expecting more than Mary Fran was capable of. At those times the expression, "Don't hurry, but just keep moving" would be used to let Mary Fran know that she didn't have to compete with anyone else. For sometimes her frustration was obvious, and very real, as she tried desperately to keep up with us but could never quite do it.

At other times the thing that was obvious was Mary Fran's great talent as an actress. When she had spent the morning playing and would then be questioned about why she wasn't ready or why her bed wasn't made, she would insist with heart-tugging sincerity, "But me *hurrying*." At those times the phrase "keep moving" would be applied as a reminder that big brown eyes and glibness aside, it was the completed project that mattered.

CHAPTER 5

Our parents quickly became accustomed to Mary Fran's unique speech difficulties. They often repeated her comments or described her adventures. They so much wanted others to know that, even though her academic skills were limited, she was a lively child capable of humor and insight.

She grew out of her seizures, as many children do. And as she grew her developmental lag wasn't so obvious. People would instead comment on her cheerful energy or long, shiny curls. There is a snapshot that must have been taken around this time. She was about six and had long, wavy auburn hair and a Kodak-perfect little-girl face. Around her sat Philip, who was fourteen, and ten-year-old Patricia. And I, a smiling four-year-old, sat nearby.

But there would come a time when her difference again stood out. At restaurants, reading menus to her no longer would look appropriate, considering her size. The coming years only increased the gap. While others her age were learning how to drive, she would still have to be driven places.

She would stay home while peers made their first break away through summer jobs out of town.

But my parents didn't know that then. They did know that Mary Fran had reached the point where she needed more than they could give her. She was seven years old when they enrolled her in her first school—a Catholic residential school for mentally retarded girls.

Our Lady of Providence was a small private school out in the country, around 200 miles from our home. It didn't seem that different from St. John's, the school that Philip, Patricia, and I went to. Mary Fran's teachers would be nuns, like ours. And like our classrooms, hers was decorated with the bright drawings and prize-winning schoolwork of the students. But the thing I was concerned about, as a five-year-old, was the playground equipment. And there it was in the back of the school, a spacious grassy area covered with colorful jungle-gym equipment. It was much more than my school had. I felt great pangs of jealousy.

Mary Fran and I had always played together. Even in my year in kindergarten I didn't meet anyone I liked as much. I didn't want to see her only on the weekends and in the summer. To lose my best friend would be horrible. Especially if she were going to get the better end of the deal. And from the look of that jungle-gym equipment, I was sure she was.

During the past few months Mom and Mary Fran had shopped for new school clothes. Our parents had frequently assured us, and themselves, that the new school was indeed going to be a treat for Mary Fran. The situation was difficult for all of us. But no one said that.

The day finally came. Name tags had been carefully sewn on her new clothes and everything was packed in the waiting station wagon. That morning, Mary Fran and I got into a fight in our bedroom while we were getting dressed. I don't remember how it started. But I remember what I said. I was very angry, and spewed out at her, "I hate you. I'm glad you're going away to school!" I felt as if I had thrown some horrible curse at her. Her eyes widened in surprise. Then she tossed her head defiantly and said, "Me glad, too!" And with that, she quickly put on her last shoe, and strode out of the room.

The other memories come back in jagged pieces: Mary Fran's teacher, a smiling nun, greeting us; being shown her bed and dresser in the dormitory; and the teacher telling my parents to give her a month to adjust before the next visit. But the thing I have always clearly remembered was seeing her trying to break out of her teacher's arms as tears streamed down her face, and she screamed for us to come back.

When we got home we all waited out the month in our own individual ways. Our father seemed to be working late at his office more often. And Philip and Patricia busied themselves with school activities. Mom seemed to be doing one load of wash after another. I don't know how she found enough dirty clothes to wash. But I spent time in the basement with her. I would sit cross-legged on the floor and work on dime store workbooks.

As I sat working on a connect-a-dot drawing one day, Mom called out, "Maureen, go upstairs and bring down any dirty clothes from your bedroom." The drawing was getting hard. I was into the high numbers, and was just improvising, so I gladly put the workbook down and ran upstairs. In my bedroom I scrounged around, finding stray socks and underwear, and a sweat shirt. As I returned with the dirty clothes Mom looked relieved, and began to sort it. She picked up my "St. John's Fighting Irish" sweat shirt. Though it was mine, Mary Fran was the one who usually wore it.

"Well, she has her own school now," Mom said softly as she held the sweat shirt.

"But I bet she'll still wear it," I said quickly. "When she comes home, I mean."

"She should have her own," Mom answered. And with that she held up the dirt-smudged and food-stained sweat shirt with the smirking leprechaun on it.

"How about this?" she asked tracing an arc over the leprechaun's head, "OUR LADY OF . . . " and then she traced along the bottom of the sweat shirt and finished proudly, " . . . PROVIDENCE!"

We both pictured the imaginary sweat shirt and began to laugh. The idea of that saintly title printed on a sweat shirt, especially with the impish leprechaun, seemed so ridiculous. Maybe it was also the release of someone's finally mentioning the school. We continued to laugh, occasionally stopping to retrace the words. Then Mom tossed the sweat shirt into the wash and said seriously, "Yes, I think she should have her own."

I imagine the school principal didn't know what to make of this new mother. In response to Mom's long distance phone call the Mother Superior said, "Yes, Mrs. Lynch. I do think the idea of an 'Our Lady of Providence' shirt is quite . . . interesting. I see by my file that you'll be visiting Mary Frances in two weeks. So why don't we say that if you are still interested in this venture, we can talk about it then . . . *sweat* shirts, yes, of course, I understand. . . . Yes, she's doing fine. Good-bye, Mrs. Lynch."

Eventually Mom and the Mother Superior were to come to an agreement. A limited number of light blue, long-sleeved "Our Lady of Providence" sweat shirts would be printed up at my parents' expense. Those not snatched up by the family would be offered for sale at the Christmas bazaar. The Mother Superior seemed almost pleased with the line drawing of the school that was printed on the sweat shirt between the lettering. "But," she warned Mom, "I don't really know if any of the other parents will be interested."

Mom, an untiring optimist, busied herself preparing order blanks for the many requests she anticipated. As it turned out, there were many orders. In fact, Mom ran out of order blanks and had to borrow notebook paper from the Mother Superior, who watched the whole scene with a rather bewildered look of pride.

After the first month, Mary Fran came home every other weekend. The pattern was always the same. On Fridays Mom would leave for Our Lady of Providence around noon. By the time she got there, classes would be over, and Mary Fran would be waiting with her suitcase packed. As she rushed to the car, Mary Fran's face would show her excitement about the approaching weekend, as well as relief that once again her mother *had* come. Despite the fact that the pattern went on for seven years with little change, Mary Fran would always stand tensely with her suitcase nearby and a worried look on her young face as she waited to be picked up on the alternate Fridays.

When they arrived home around seven o'clock we would sit down to dinner together. These Friday night dinners were stilted at first. We felt that it was the beginning of a special weekend. We certainly couldn't waste it talking about every-day things, as we usually did. But if we didn't, what would we talk about? Eventually everything settled into place. And after the initial edginess, things became as predictable as the fish sticks we had every Friday night for dinner.

Saturday the clock seemed to be racing at double time. And Sunday morning we all woke knowing what would happen. We'd leave for school early in the morning, and stop halfway to go to Mass. The atmosphere was a festive, Sunday-outing feeling. And as we got closer to Our Lady of Providence we all strained to keep it that way. After deciding on a restaurant, we would stop for lunch. In warm weather this was usually replaced by a picnic, something Mary Fran anticipated with glee.

But as we neared the small town ten miles from school, her mood would change drastically, as if she suddenly remembered what the whole trip was about. Her face would whiten as she nervously checked the passing scenery, yes, this was certainly it; her school was near. Usually her sweaty hands would reach out to Mom as she asked to stop at a gas station—one last bottle of soda, one last trip to the bathroom, one last anything.

Dreading the last few miles as much as we were, our parents usually agreed to stop. And we would all loiter at the gas station until every possible activity had been exhausted. Once more entering the car, blaming it for bringing us there, we drove the remaining miles in silence.

The silence was always broken by Mary Fran's cry, "Mom!" And Mom would turn to help her as she vomited. By now, Dad had turned into the driveway of the school. And the sounds of Mary Fran's throwing up and Mom's voice trying to calm her were accompanied by the sharp sounds of the tires pushing determinedly up the driveway and sending the gravel flying.

We all entered the school quietly, with occasional remarks about the weekend's high points and promises about the next weekend home. Often Mary Fran would throw up again on the tiled foyer. Patricia and I would be sent off to the bathroom for paper towels, and Mom and Sister Regina would rush to clean up the floor. Fast kisses, promises, tears. And we were in the car again, this time without Mary Fran, heading home.

Those Sundays always confused me. I wanted to take Mary Fran aside in the morning and remind her what came after the picnic. Maybe we could run away, anything so we wouldn't have to go through another Sunday with its determined cheerfulness one minute and raw pain the next. At the restaurant, I'd look at Mary Fran's plate of food and try to figure out what color stain it was going to leave on the car. I hated seeing my parents' false excitement during the meal, and frozen smiles as they said good-bye to the nun who held my screaming sister. I just wanted Mom and Dad to say that they were as angry as I was that Mary Fran couldn't stay home like everybody else.

Summer was the one time that this schedule changed. Then she came home for three months straight. The weekends came and went unthreateningly. This luxury was made even better by the knowledge that we would move to our cottage for the summer. It was in South Haven, about thirty miles from where we lived, a sturdy little wood-frame house with Lake Michigan in our front yard, and acres and acres of wild woods as our back yard.

Memorial Day heralded the end of the school year. And the end of the school year meant the same thing to all of us: moving to the cottage. Mary Fran was the first one out of school. And she loved the position of being Mom's main helper as summer clothes were packed and everything readied. Once the rest of us finished school the excitement was unbearable. We grew impatient with our parents' double-checking of clothes and supplies. At many points we were ready to leave them and walk to the cottage. We were sure we'd get there sooner. But that would mean not being involved in the race, and in this particular case, getting there really was half the fun.

With the building of a slick triple lane highway, two ways of getting to our cottage had become available. The old road traveled near Lake Michigan and wound through groves of trees with a constant no-passing stripe down its center. It was a beautiful route, but sometimes it would be clogged by tractors or other farm machinery. The new road was straighter and, with the multiple lanes, it offered the suggestion of being speedier. Our mother insisted it wasn't, that the old road was still the best. And so the battle began.

Our father merely scoffed at her and squeezed into the tiny Karmann-Ghia he used for zipping to his office. Not to be outdone, our mother slid behind the wheel of the dependable green station wagon that was stuffed with boxes of summer clothes and a panting—and very impatient—collie, Lady. Mom glanced down at the dashboard with all the panache of a professional racing car driver. Then she looked over at us. Dad watched us, too. And there the four of us stood trying to decide who was the best bet.

Weighing all the angles, we finally made our decision. It varied from year to year. Sometimes Philip rushed to ride with Dad. And it would turn into a battle of the sexes as Mom, Patricia, Mary Fran, Lady, and I chugged along in the station wagon. At those times Mary Fran and I would sit in the back with Lady who would lick us generously in her excitement. Lady was even more impatient than we were.

Once there, she would beg to be let out at the end of the long, winding driveway so she could run through the woods and up to the house. The winner was never the same. But regardless of who won, it was driving up the quarter-mile driveway that was the most exciting. We'd strain to see through the tangle of trees looking for the glint of sunlight off of a car window or piece of chrome.

Once we got there, deciding what to do first tied us up. Should we jump in the lake, run up the sand dunes, or explore the woods? We calmed down once we realized that we would have three months with nothing to do but play. There would be plenty of time to do everything. But that naive judgment underestimated our zealous parents.

From the way Dad directed his troop of four, one would have thought he was a professional army captain, even though he had never spent a day in the service due to his high blood pressure. But he laid out his directions, explicit and demanding, each morning before driving to his office. And there was no question in anyone's mind that the first concern of the day would be completing our recently administered duties.

Our parents had bought the cottage at a time when lake property was inexpensive. The local residents saw little of value in the wooded thirteen acres. They were aware of the damage caused by the harsh winters and severe lake storms. To them, the long winding driveway through the woods meant waist-high drifts of snow and frozen ice that would necessitate being plowed out every morning once the long winter season began. And the lake view only meant erosion, as well as the rebuilding of beach stairs every year as storms dismantled the current stairs and spewed the lumber along the shore.

But our parents dug in with delight. Soon the grapevines that had blocked the lake view were dug up and grass was planted in their place. Plumbing was put in and the electrical wiring was patched up. It was done slowly, every summer a new project. Eventually it seemed that everything that could be done was done. That was when our parents introduced us to a new concept—maintenance.

If our father was the captain, our mother was the efficient and equally demanding battalion leader. Though her family had moved to South Haven when she was a teenager, she had grown up on a sheep ranch in the Black Hills. So she was not one to take chores lightly. Together our parents would decide on priorities. Our father would give us the assignments before zipping down the driveway to his office in nearby Benton Harbor. And our mother was there to make sure we didn't go back to bed. She would prod us on by assuring us that if we really worked hard we could finish by noon. Sometimes we did. Other times the day dragged on, and we'd complain that we'd get everything done just in time to go back to school. Our father would answer that he hoped so because he'd hate to see us miss the first month of classes.

Our time was usually taken with mowing the lawn, chopping out weeds, pruning the trees, raking dead fish off the beach, filling up holes in the driveway, and other forms of the much-cursed maintenance. Since Philip was the oldest and strongest, he was the boss of each work site. Patricia wasn't far from the top herself. But Mary Fran and I were out-and-out serfs. It was our job to do the stooping, picking, and running.

When we weren't stooping, picking, and running we played with the pets, or created sand masterpieces on the beach. An unbiased outsider would probably report that despite all our complaints about chores, a great deal of time was spent in playing. We would be accompanied by any one of the family's turtles, rabbits, horses, dogs, and cats.

The summer that our cat had kittens, Mary Fran quickly found the way to their heart by catching grasshoppers for them. The poor grasshoppers were no match for her. That summer she was constantly followed by the mother and her six chubby kittens. They devotedly followed her in a straight line until she'd suddenly break from them to begin her grasshopper-catching dance. I don't know how she originally thought of it. But none of the rest of us seemed to have her talent as a grasshopper-catcher. So the cats stayed with her. And she would stay with them until they lay about her on the grass in swollen-bellied contentment.

The summer after I finished second grade I looked forward to showing Mary Fran everything I had learned about reading. I guess I thought it was an oversight on her teachers' part that she wasn't being taught to read like I was. So I dragged out the beginning readers. We sat together on a grassy hill overlooking the lake as I drilled her on sounding out the words. I tried to remember how Sister Jarleth had taught us so I could use the same technique.

Mary Fran played the dutiful student. Though she was willing and hard-working we always seemed to get distracted. The books would be left behind as we went on to a different game, something that we were both good at. Nevertheless, we seemed to make an annual attempt at reading, an attempt to bridge the gap that was developing between us.

CHAPTER 6

Memories from the early years often popped up during our year in Seattle; though there was a great deal of introspection, I was most concerned about the present. Philip had spent a whole week with us when we were trying to find a house to rent. But he and Betty were busy with their own concerns. Most of their friends were married couples in their thirties with whom Mary Fran and I had little in common. So we latched on to our own version of the welcome wagon–the Kiwanis Center.

The Kiwanis Center was a social-recreational program for mentally retarded adults. Though the local Kiwanis Club intended the building to function as a drop-in center, it also housed three social workers who ran an information center.

The social workers' offices were squeezed off to one corner of the building. Space was at a premium, and it was obvious that the many activities the center offered had priority over the office work. A schedule was posted which announced that the center was open daily from three to ten. For those who couldn't read, colorful posters were drawn to announce classes in things like cooking, macrame, and money management. There were the favorites that no one had to be reminded about—the Know Your Community Tours, Wednesday night supper club, and Saturday night at the movies.

Since the Center was downtown, near main bus lines, it was easily accessible. But the people who went there were so dedicated, I think they would have found their way, buses or no buses. Most of them were young, in their twenties and thirties. They would all be classified as mentally retarded. But that's where the similarities stopped. Some of them lived with their families, some in their own apartments, and some in group homes. Some of them arrived shortly after three, having gone straight from the sheltered workshop. And other people, those who were in competitive employment, arrived around six o'clock, after leaving their jobs. But they all had one thing in mind—going to a place where they could enjoy themselves with friends. A place where they wouldn't be treated as students, clients, or residents; just a place to be themselves, a place of their own.

On our first visit, Pat Mitchell, the center's director, greeted us. Pat was an easygoing young woman with short blonde hair who looked closer to twelve years-old than her twenty-five. Her unassuming manner was perfect for the center, but it belied the obvious disciplined organizational talents that were necessary to set up the more than fifteen activities that were held every week. She told us the center's only two rules—hang up your coat in the front, and if you want to join the Wednesday night supper club you have to sign up a week in advance.

We wandered around from room to room. In one, a group of people sat and talked; some smoked and everyone had a can of soda. They looked up at us briefly without stopping their conversations. In the next room two people played pool while another group sat in the corner quietly working on their money management assignment. Everyone else was in the back room, scattered around on the floor. They were working on decorations for next week's dance—a sock hop, Pat told us. She had followed us into the back room and didn't seem satisfied with our attempt to mingle. I gladly grabbed construction paper and felt pens after she suggested that I might want to help.

With one sister settled, Pat then turned to the other: "How about a game of pool, Mary Fran?"

"O.K.," she answered shyly while glancing over at me.

They walked into the next room together. Mary Fran walked quickly with a self-conscious stoop of the shoulders. But she had a wide smile on her face that told Pat pool was the right choice.

When it was time to leave I asked Pat where we could catch the number seventeen bus that took us two blocks from our house. I had looked at the map earlier and saw that a bus stop was on the corner of the Kiwanis Center. But I wanted Mary Fran to see me asking for directions. I wanted us to learn together. Mary Fran watched Pat as she told us where to catch the bus, and her face registered admiration for her new friend.

The next day we went to the Kiwanis Center again. This time I had an appointment with Jane Selby, one of the social workers. I was hoping that Jane could give us ideas about job training programs. She invited me into her office, and I tried to explain what we wanted. As I talked, I watched her face closely, trying to find out what she was thinking. I kept hoping that she wouldn't say what we were doing was a peculiar idea, or impossible, or that I was a "very special person." The appointments I had had with agencies the past month had resulted in little but such comments. I was tired of being made to feel strange or saintly.

Jane pulled a sheet of paper out of her desk and reached over to her card file. "These should give you something to start with," she told me as she wrote. Her list included a nursery school teacher's aid training program, a food service program, and two sheltered workshops that she assured me had more jobs than just sanding wood.

After I took the list I tried to describe Mary Fran to Jane. I wanted her to know that she was capable, that she was worth believing in. Then I added, "When I was little my parents used to always quote her and I'd get so jealous. But now I do the same thing. I've been carrying little anecdotes with me as if they were precious jewels. As if all I have to do is flash them at social workers or teachers and they will suddenly understand her true worth."

Jane laughed, "I do the same thing with my clients! The frustrating thing is no one ever seems to appreciate the stories like I hope they will."

I must have thanked Jane ten times as I left; just as much for what she didn't say as for what she did. It wasn't that I don't like compliments. It was wonderful to get encouragement. The social workers at the Kiwanis Center were such a boost . . . John Cozzolino's wink as he smiled and said, "Go get 'em, kid!" Or Jane's willingness to constantly provide us with new job leads. Or even the implicit trust when some of the families I met told me their stories. Those were people I respected, and whose motives I didn't have to question.

But what I distrusted was meeting someone whose job it was to provide services when all they did was babble noncommital generalizations or sugary praises. I always ended up thinking, you're making a living off of my sister, and our family, and others like us. And you're not giving us anything in return.

My brother would probably accuse me of being unreasonable. I imagine he'd remind me that the people whose desks I would gladly set on fire are just as caught in a bind as everyone else. They can't find someone a job when jobs don't exist. They can't open group homes when neighborhoods continue to hide behind zoning regulations. He's right. I'm sure he must be right. But if that's true, why is it that some people manage; what secret do the Jane Selbys and John Cozzolinos have. What is it that keeps them going?

Later that week Christina arrived. She had gotten a car in Chicago from a company that paired up people who wanted to get their cars to other cities with people who would drive them. The car Christina had been given was stuffed with clothes, books, rugs, lamps, and dishes. She came jumping out of the car in a Carleton College T-shirt and cut-offs.

After a quick greeting she said, "What time is it? They're really strict about the car being delivered on time. I think I better get it over to the garage."

"Come on in the house," I said, "And I'll check the time." Pointing proudly to the house, I quickly added, "Well, what do you think? Is it what you thought it would look like?"

Mary Fran and I waited on the sidewalk as Christina looked up at the house. "How did you ever find it?" she asked. "It's wonderful!"

We smiled smugly as we followed her up the steps that led to the front yard. "We like it," I said. "That's what our mom used to always say when someone complimented her on our house—'Well . . . we like it.' "

Christina was already in the house. "Oh, how nice," she said, "window seats!"

"A stylish elegance paired with the simplicity of another era," I said.

"You sound like those sections in Sunday magazines," she said. "You know where they have pictures of different people's homes each week."

"I wanted to talk to you about that," I said. "I think we have a good chance of making it in the *Seattle Times.*"

Christina looked into the kitchen where the only furniture was an uneven card table and three lawn chairs. In the living room we had an antique oak table Philip had loaned us. The only other piece of furniture was a worn, corduroy-covered chair in the corner that Betty had helped us bring home from a garage sale.

"Well, they certainly won't be able to accuse us of being ostentatious," Christina said.

"We never said we were finished," I said. "In fact, we purposely waited with the major decorating decisions until you got here."

"We could make pillows for the window seats," she said.

"I wasn't being quite as ambitious," I admitted. "I was thinking more along the line of splurging on curtains."

"I think I have some material that would be good for that," she said. "It's out in the car. And I brought some lamps, too."

"All that stuff in the car is yours?" I asked.

"I started out very organized," Christina explained. "But my parents kept adding things . . . I kept trying to convince them that Seattle couldn't be that different from Chicago; that they must have can openers and extension cords and garlic presses there, too."

It took us about half an hour to drag all the boxes and packages inside. Then Christina left to return the car. And Mary Fran and I sat in our newly cluttered home.

I looked at all the boxes in amazement. It was typical of Christina, an expert in organizing softball games and designing handmade quilts, to come prepared. I should have known that she would come with a carload of things ranging from lamps to a garlic press.

She had said she stopped at her relatives in South Dakota for a few days before driving on to Seattle. She had grown up on a farm there. After her father finished ministry school in Chicago, he took his city bride back to South Dakota. They worked on the family farm, and had four children. I think Christina said that she was in junior high school when they left it for Chicago, before eventually moving to a small town outside of Chicago where her father was the high school guidance counselor.

I wondered what her family thought of her coming here for a year. It was early October and we had been waiting a month for her decision. It had seemed like they were worried about her going all the way to the West Coast. She had told me that her mother didn't think it was practical when she didn't have any idea if she could get a job. But Christina, who had just graduated in June, assured them that the kind of job she got didn't matter. She wanted a break before going to graduate school, and she'd settle for any kind of work.

Actually having her there seemed strange. Her younger sister, Ingrid, was my roommate in college. But Christina and I had only been together when we'd both happen to be at the cafeteria at the same time, or have short talks if we were both leaving the dorm to go to classes. When Christina was a junior and well-established with her group of friends and interests, we were just starting. As freshmen we spent most of our time trying to act calm, and secretly fearing that our own acceptance had been a computer error.

Ingrid had been the one who suggested that Christina live with us. The last two weeks of August, when I had been home in Michigan, Ingrid and Christina came to visit for a weekend. As we walked on the beach, I briefly mentioned that I would probably be taking the year off from school. I wasn't that sure about it myself, and talking about it with others only seemed to make it more complicated.

At first their reaction was disbelief. They came from a family where everything always seemed to make sense. Their parents had high expectations for their children; and their mother worked hard to keep their life orderly and predictable. Ingrid had once bragged that their mother toilet trained them all at an early age simply by saying "Diapers are disgusting. I'm sure you'd be much more comfortable using the toilet." And that had been that. Ingrid always insisted that was a true story. And no matter how much we'd ask for Christina's memories, she would always just smile at Ingrid's animation and refuse to disagree.

Though they had been surprised at my change of plans, Ingrid soon joined in with a sort of hysterical excitement that she always had when she smelled spontaneity in the air. "Though it must be a difficult decision," she had said, "I think it sounds wonderful. In fact, Christina's been wondering what to do . . . and she mentioned wanting to live in the Northwest. Christina, why don't you go there, too? It could be fantastic!"

Knowing that she could depend on spending two more years at Carleton College, Ingrid abandoned herself to planning our next year. And Mary Fran's year, too. But Mary Fran wasn't with us that day. She was camping in Seattle, and would be returning soon with Mom. Christina had met her briefly at Carleton when she and Mom had visited. But neither one of them remembered much about each other.

"You like this lamp?" Fran asked pointing to the pile of Christina's things that took up most of the dining room. I suddenly felt very wary about the three of us living together. Please Fran, I thought to myself, if you're going to do anything strange, don't do it when Christina's around.

But we actually saw very little of Christina. She soon settled into her own schedule and was kept busy trying to find a job. We worked at home during the day while she was out job hunting. And during the night while we went to classes, Christina relaxed at home and planned her next day's strategy. But I asked her help when I thought Fran should finally travel alone by bus.

Busing home would be much less scary than busing downtown. So I planned to meet Mary Fran at the Kiwanis Center after her math tutoring, and wait with her for the bus. As soon as the bus left I'd call Christina at home, and she would be at the bus stop when Mary Fran got off. Christina was confident there would be no problems, Mary Fran was concerned there might be, and I was in a pure panic.

The night was rainy and blustery. It was the middle of October, and the record-breaking sunny days of the past month were long gone. We waited at the bus stop, and I reminded Mary Fran that I was going to take the University bus. After a full day together, we looked forward to our separate evenings when she went to the Kiwanis Center, and I went to an extension class at the University.

We finally saw the bus turn the corner. "Look, here it comes," I said.

"You come with me," she said, "just this last time." Seeing that the plea had no effect, she added quickly, "Tell me again, Mo. What street me get off on?"

"Seventy-first," I answered, "And I'll ask the driver to remind you when he gets there."

As the bus pulled away from the curb I watched it turn the corner before rushing down the street to a telephone booth. I was sure Mary Fran's bus would be in our neighborhood before I even got a dime out of my purse.

Christina answered the phone and assured me, "Maureen, I promise! I'll be waiting at the bus stop in twenty-five minutes. Now go to your class, and *relax*."

As I was to find out later, twenty-five minutes from my call Mary Fran walked self-assuredly in the door just as Christina was getting ready to go to the bus stop. I had felt our twice-a-day trips for the past month had prepared Mary Fran to go alone. But I was also concerned. It was such an important step in becoming independent, but could she learn to tell the right street, the right bus, or make correct change?

Her years of being a nonreader in a world full of signs had taught her ways of compensating. Just as she shops by recognizing logos and box designs, she remembered buildings instead of street names. When a bus came, she ignored the slew of letters and looked straight at the red numbers, knowing she wanted number seventeen, and she remembered that she needed a nickel and a quarter. I was thrilled.

A call to our mother resulted in maternal concern: "Are you sure she's ready for this? What if . . . " Having elaborated on an amazing list of situations, a storehouse that only parents seem to have access to, she became more enthusiastic, and she declared, "I thought she could."

Always having had to rely on other people, Mary Fran was suddenly able to come and go as she chose. The change this made in her went beyond the new skill itself. It was as if she realized that since she could do this—something that had always been so confusingly exotic—maybe she could do other things, too. No longer the passive student, she began to talk about things she wanted to learn, and jobs she wanted to train for. It was quite a change to get used to.

CHAPTER 7

One afternoon I returned home from an errand to find the house empty. I paced around telling myself that this was fabulous; Mary Fran had gotten bored, and had gone for a walk. Or maybe she had decided to get some groceries. What growth, I marveled, trying to convince myself. Then I saw her through the window, as she walked toward our house, carrying a laundry bag. I rushed onto the porch and demanded, "Fran, where were you?"

"Doing my dirty clothes," she answered as she walked past me into the house.

"Well . . . well, why didn't you leave a note?" I stammered.

Mary Fran was halfway up the stairs with her laundry when she turned to drawl out in impatience, "Mo!" Then, seeing my frantic mood, she added, "You know me can't write."

Most of Mary Fran's accomplishments sneaked up on us. They usually emerged from a quick decision on her part, or a disagreement between us. One night I found myself having an argument with her about calling a friend. I insisted it was too late, I told her it was already 12:30. But Mary Fran was adamant; she had to make the call. Then I remembered that only a month earlier I had to practically force her to take the phone long enough to even say "hello" to Philip when he called. Never knowing if the person on the other end would understand her, Mary Fran had always tried to ignore the telephone.

I guess that's the way she felt about talking to strangers, too. It had become easier to just sit passively during dinners or parties, saving her comments and questions for later when only her family was left.

Mary Fran and I decided that if she were going to look for a job, she would have to have a résumé. "A résumé is something you take with you when you're applying for a job," I explained to Mary Fran. "It's a piece of paper that tells your name, address, what schools you went to, and if you've ever had a job before."

"Arlington not count," Mary Fran said half as a statement, half as a question, naming the sheltered workshop she had attended in Michigan. Her face looked pinched, and she seemed ready to blame me for her frustrations at Arlington.

"You're right," I agreed. "Arlington doesn't count as a job. But you can list it under your schools, right after Our Lady of Providence."

I reached for a writing tablet and pretended to be an aloof interviewer. "All right now, your name please?" I asked.

"Mary," she answered.

"Tsk, tsk, only one name, it's a pity but I'm afraid we don't hire people who only have one name," I said while ripping up the sheet of paper.

Mary Fran laughed and said, "Mo, you know my last name!" Thinking that a clue might help, she added, "It's the same as yours."

"Fran! You have to pretend we don't know each other," I explained. "Pretend you came into my office because I needed to hire someone for a really good job that you'd love to have, like a . . . "

"Waitress!" she said quickly. "Like Trish," she added naming our sister.

"Okay, a waitress," I agreed, trying not to show my disappointment with her career ideal. "Now . . . the kinds of questions someone would ask you are real simple, they're just questions about yourself. Ready to start?"

"Okay," she agreed hesitantly.

"Your name please, Miss?" I asked.

"Mary Lynch," she answered.

"Mary, okay, how do you spell your last name?"

"Here," she said reaching for my tablet. "Me do it." She took my pen and wrote in purposeful block letters "L-Y-N-C-H."

"Thank you, dear," I told her. "And what is your address, Miss Lynch?"

"Mo," she whispered leaning forward as if trying to talk around the me that was interviewing her, "Mo, I don't know our address yet."

"Well, Miss Lynch, do you happen to have it written down, in your purse or pocket?" I asked.

Mary Fran remembered the picture I.D. we had gotten after the incident with the spilt groceries. She kept it in her coat pocket along with a number 17 bus schedule and an extra dime in case she had to call home. There were times when she would forget and leave her bus schedule or I.D. at home. I was always reminding her about it.

"Yes, it's in my pocket," she answered impatiently as if I were checking up on her. "And have a bus schedule, too."

Her voice was edgy so I thought maybe we should take some time off. "Fran, look outside," I said. "It's cleared up. Why don't we take off and go run?"

"No, you run," she answered, "Me work on my 'zumé."

I had started running in high school when a group of us organized Special Olympic meets in our area. Since then I had been hooked. But Mary Fran, even though she had won many events at local and state Special Olympic meets, could always think of other things she'd rather do.

"Okay, if you're going to keep working on your résumé let me write down our address," I said, bending over the writing tablet. "Um, what else do you need, 'schools attended' and . . . "

"Your typewriter," Mary Fran added.

"It's in my bedroom," I answered. "I'll bring it down after I change clothes." I ran up the stairs to my bedroom. I had thought she would just print her résumé. But if she wanted to try the typewriter I wasn't going to say no.

I put on some track shorts and a T-shirt and took the typewriter downstairs. Mary Fran said good-bye in an unconcerned way, and I closed the door behind me and jumped down our front steps. The sudden appearance of the sun had changed the Saturday morning that had started out being typically gray and drizzly. It was a warm October day that brought out mothers pushing strollers. We were an oddity in our family-oriented neighborhood of large old houses, well-groomed yards, and Volvo station wagons.

Our neighbors had looked us over and decided that we were students. "How's school?" they'd sometimes call to us. We appreciated their friendliness and it was usually easier to answer "fine" than to try to explain what we really were doing. I ran along the sidewalk passing backyards full of blonde kids and red rhododendrons. We lived in Ballard, Seattle's Scandinavian neighborhood. Christina wasn't as interested in the Scandinavian food shops as we were. They just reminded her of her family's holiday dinners. But the gjetost and lefsa and ludfisk were all new to Mary Fran and me.

As I ran down the hillside that our house was on I could see the fishing ships docked in the Ballard Bay. My shoulders and neck felt like someone was behind me, digging fingers into my muscles. It had been a bad week and, whether I admitted it to myself or not, my body seemed determined to remind me. As I turned on to the road that wound along the bay to the Marina I let my head drop. Moving it to both sides I could hear the joints cracking like flying gravel. But as I continued down the street my muscles gradually began to feel less tight.

We had begun the week with a long list of jobs to check out. We used the list of training programs that Jane, the social worker at the Kiwanis Center, had given us. And we supplemented it with ads from the neighborhood newspaper; ads for jobs like aides in hospitals and rest homes, kitchen helpers, or maintenance staff. It seemed like the most reasonable next step, since during the past months, when we had gone the conventional route of agencies, we had ended up shuttling back and forth among the offices.

But by the second day we weren't sure this was any better. Jobs were scarce, and these previously "undesirable" occupations had many people competing for them. At many of the rest homes that advertised for maintenance staff, Mary Fran was competing with college students and housewives.

We knew how hard it was to get a job because even Christina was having trouble. She had thought of this year as being a break before beginning graduate school in classics at the University of Chicago. She wasn't picky about a job; she was willing to take almost anything that she could support herself on. But the statistics about unemployed liberal arts graduates were becoming more real to her. Every morning she put on the same skirt and blazer, her interview outfit. With a city transit map in one hand and the help wanted ads in the other she would start out, still remembering the comments at the employment agency the last week.

"Nope, nothing for classics majors today," the man at the agency had told her. "Seriously, honey, the big thing we get requests for are R.N.'s and people with accounting and business skills. Do you know how to type?"

At the end of the day the three of us would straggle home for an evening of arguing about who would shop for groceries, how we'd split household expenses, and when we'd cook. The fact that we were in a strange city, unemployed and afraid we'd stay that way, remained unspoken. Instead we argued about things like the use of honey versus sugar with a ferociousness that surprised us.

I hoped we could find something soon. Mary Fran's newborn confidence about being able to bus alone was being worn away by the numerous daily job rejections. Mary Fran had never been to parties where one of the first questions was "What do you do?" And she wasn't given to sociological monologues on people's identities being defined by their jobs. But she knew very well how important a job was.

She became unsettled by our lack of success. I imagine her feelings reminded her of her frustrations the past years at Arlington Workshop. During our daily rounds Mary Fran would frequently use the word that she had overhead teachers using when discussing students—"capable." Mary Fran understood the power of it, she knew that depending on how it was used in reports and evaluations, it shaped people's lives. For years she heard it being used about her—"She's capable," "She isn't capable" . . .

Now she grabbed at the word herself, using it as if trying to rid herself of those ghosts, and assert herself among these strangers. Never during an interview, but often during the day Mary Fran would turn to me and insist, "Me capable. Some people at my school not. But me *capable!*"

The thing that worried me most was when she didn't even bother to look at me and say it fightingly. But she continued to say the words, looking down at the ground like a dejected street bum. At times like that I couldn't stand it, and would spurt out with some ridiculously optimistic prediction. Knowing how much she liked parties and cooking I once said, "You'll get a job! And when you do we'll have Philip and Betty over, and maybe some people from the Kiwanis Center. And we'll get wine and cook a lot of good stuff. Won't that be neat, Fran?"

She didn't say anything at first, then she looked at me angrily and said "Why? Why be so special if me get job? We don't have a party when you get jobs."

Since employers had their pick of people, the attitude we

kept facing was an echo of the social work professor's comment when I spoke to her about the baby-sitting job. "Why should I hire you two," she had said, "when I can get thousands of other girls who don't have to bring their retarded sisters along?" The rest home employers, who in the past would look for strong, punctual, hardworking people, had suddenly begun to check college credentials. It seemed that Mary Fran and I were able to get just so far, to get teased on by one accomplishment, only to find ourselves back at the beginning again.

As I thought of that, my pulse beat faster and I realized that my pace had quickened as I ran along the street. Ballard was behind me and I was running along the shoulder of the street that led to the Leif Erickson Marina. I could see two women in the distance running toward me; they lived across the street from us. I recognized them as the mothers of some of the kids I had passed in the beginning of my run. They smiled and we exchanged quick, jerky waves before going on our separate ways.

My thoughts returned to the past week. And I remembered how relieved we had all been on Wednesday. The perfect job, it seemed, had fallen into Mary Fran's lap. The day before, we had decided to put aside the Help Wanted ads in favor of one of the training programs that Jane from the Kiwanis Center had told us about. She had mentioned a day care center, Happy Faces, whose director was interested in starting a training program for teachers' aides. Jane wasn't sure if the program had started. But she knew the director, who was working on his doctorate in special education, had contacted the Division of Vocational Rehabilitation about obtaining funding. Jane had heard that it would be a four-month training program with minimum wage, followed by help in finding a full-time teacher's aide job.

Mary Fran didn't believe me when I told her about it. She looked at me with impatience and said, "Not without high school, Mo. Have to have high school degree. Me don't."

She said the words "high school" with the mixed anger and

respect of an outsider. When we were living at home to-gether, the local public high school I went to had signified everything that her county-based special education school lacked. South Haven Public High School glittered with an unattainable normality that included band concerts, football games, and foreign language classes. And I flitted in and out of everything.

When I was in eleventh grade my Spanish class had been preparing for the school's open house. After school we met at my house to work on piñatas. After the group of giggly teenagers had left Mary Fran came into the living room where I was cleaning up. She asked me why there weren't Spanish classes at her school like there were at mine. Before I could say anything she answered, "Oh, it's because we're too dumb." She had said it angrily as if daring me to deny that it was the reason. Then she left me wishing that my SAT scores were lower, as I picked the crepe paper off the living room floor.

We circled gingerly around each other during those years. But both of us felt betrayed. After seven years at Our Lady of Providence, Mary Fran had returned home to go to the local special education school that the public school system had begun to offer. Our teenage selves realized that it wasn't the same as when we were little, before either of us had gone to school. I had felt like dropping the crepe paper and run-ning after her to shout, "Yes, I have friends! And I like going to the high school, we do things that are fun. And I *am smart!* I can't help it."

But I didn't say any of that. I hardly even thought about it then. It was just easier that way. But I couldn't hide behind a bustling schedule this year. Mary Fran was looking surly and walking around the living room as she waited for me to answer.

"You don't need a high school diploma, Fran. That's just it. This program is for people who never went to high school. They'll teach you how to work with little kids. Then at the end you get a certificate and they help you find a job as a teacher's aide. Now, do you want to try it?"

"Yes, I guess so," she answered. "How me get there?"

"We'll have to check the transit map, but I'm sure a bus stops nearby. Jane says it's not far from the Kiwanis Center."

"Alone?" Mary Fran asked.

"No, of course not. I'll go with you until you learn the route."

The next day we were up early and ready to leave for Mary Fran's first day of work. A few calls had arranged it easily. The director of Happy Faces was delighted that we had heard about his program. He had one trainee and was trying to recruit others. He admitted that his individual classroom teachers were not completely sold on the program.

"They're great in early childhood ed.," he told me. "But they have a way to go when it comes to dealing with people who are mentally retarded. We'll win them over, though."

To get to Happy Faces we took the same bus that Mary Fran took for the Kiwanis Center. Then there was a five-block walk and we were there. It was easy to find. On the side of the building was painted a colorful clown's face. The building looked out of place on the edge of Seattle's busy downtown business district. When Jane had told me about it she had said, "It's easy to find because it's the only building on the block with a huge clown's face on the side. Just turn right on Sixth Avenue, and then keep an eye out for a protruding red nose." I had laughed at her description thinking that she was exaggerating. But she had been pretty accurate. From a distance it looked as if the nose was competing with the pedestrians for sidewalk space.

Inside, the director of the school, John Rosinski, greeted us. He was a tall, thin young man with an open friendly face. John introduced us to Suzy Chambers, the classroom teacher Mary Fran would be working with. Then he took Mary Fran for a tour of the school. I turned to Suzy, who was watching me carefully. She had brown hair with blonde streaks in it, and wore a peach-colored pant suit.

"I don't know much about special education," Suzy said to me. She continued to tell me that she had a B.A. in elementary education from Washington State University.

"Well, it sounds like your training program is going to be good," I told her.

"It's not really our program. It's John's," she answered as she busily arranged the piles of construction paper on the shelf.

Mary Fran and John returned to the classroom. And I left, saying that I'd be back at 3:00. I passed mothers who were bringing sleepy-eyed three-year-olds in the door. I wondered if any of them would be in Mary Fran's class.

Two days later, when I arrived at 3:00 to help Mary Fran bus home, John called me into his office.

"It's not working out," he told me. "Your sister is just standing, she's not doing anything. And Suzy's been complaining that she doesn't have time to tell Mary everything . . . I've already told your sister."

There was nothing I could say. He made it clear that his first responsibility was to the teachers. And that he had to find trainees who would fit in easily. You'd hardly need training, I thought, if you could fit into this place in two days. Making two wrong turns I eventually made my way to Mary Fran's classroom. She was standing stiffly near the window with her coat on.

A little boy tugged at her pant leg and repeated over and over, "Teacher, have to go potty. Teacher!"

"Fran!" I said angrily, "Take him to the bathroom."

"Where?" she asked.

"I don't know where it is, I don't work here!" I said. "Oh, come on, let's go."

We left together, and it made me mad to see that she seemed relieved to be out of the school. Damn her, it would have been so good if she had just tried. I was furious. But she didn't seem to have a care in the world as she checked her pocket for the quarter and nickel she needed for the bus ride home.

My anger was spewing out in all different directions. Where do they get off calling it a training program? He was probably just doing it so he'd have something to write his doctoral dissertation on. And that ridiculous teacher, she was comfortable with mentally retarded people if she was tutoring them in the local institution, but not if she was working with them. It was really my fault. I had dragged Mary Fran into it, determined to make her fit in. She had told me herself that she really wanted to be a waitress.

I calmed down as we got to the bus stop. And I thought of the things I could have done to make it work. But all I was left with was an armful of should-haves.

That was yesterday. The next morning Mary Fran was more than happy to have me leave to go running. I was a few blocks from home, and I slowed down to a walk so I could cool off. I vowed to myself not to take everything so intensely. It would be better for both of us if we eased up and spent more time appreciating her accomplishments.

As I walked up our front steps I heard infrequent typewriter clicks. She must still be working on her résumé, I thought, she's really determined. I opened the door and went into the kitchen where Mary Fran sat bending over the typewriter. Getting a glass of water, I looked over her shoulder at the smudged paper she was typing. There were frequent skips but I could make out her name and telephone number.

"Hey, Fran, pretty good!" I said as I took a drink of water.

She straightened up and didn't bother to look at me as she disagreed, "Is not!" To prove her point she ripped the paper out of the typewriter and got up to throw it in the garbage can.

"Well, I guess it could be a little better," I said as I thought about how ridiculous we were. One of these days we were going to agree about something.

The phone rang and I went to answer it as Mary Fran made a point of noisily straightening her chair and beginning to type again.

It was Philip on the phone. He was surprised by the

weather change and wanted us to go for a ferry ride with him and Betty to Bainbridge Island. I told him I was going to spend the afternoon stripping the paint off an old chest I had gotten at a garage sale.

"How about Fran?" he asked.

"I don't think she'll want to go either, she's working on her résumé." I told him.

"Let me talk to her anyway," he suggested.

Mary Fran took the phone and I went into the kitchen for more water. I heard her laughing and giving one word answers. When I came out she had hung up and was on her way upstairs.

"Fran, where are you going?" I called.

"On the ferry," she answered as she rummaged around in her room for coins.

I looked down at my clothes and decided I didn't have to change for the bus ride to Philip and Betty's. I could go over there with Fran and catch the next bus back. It wouldn't take more than forty minutes. But I decided to wait until she asked me; she seemed to be taking it for granted that I would go along.

Mary Fran came rushing down the steps and passed me as I sat on the window seat waiting for her. She paused at the door.

"Okay, bye Mo," she called.

"Fran, are you going alone?" I asked doing a bad job of trying to cover my surprise.

"Yeah, Philip said 'hurry.' Gotta go," she answered.

"But it's not the number seventeen bus, do you remember how to get there?" I asked. We had been to Philip and Betty's only about four times.

"Sure, walk to Ballard, then number three and two," she answered.

"That's right, but do you have a number thirty-two bus schedule with you?"

"Yes," she said pulling it out of her pocket.

"Do you know where to get off? It's tricky, remember,

right over the hill. And then you walk three blocks and turn left. They live in the brick apartment building, the brown brick . . . "

"Have to go, Mo," Mary Fran said as she ran down our front steps.

I stood on the front porch in shock. This wasn't in my lesson plan. "Have a good time, Fran!" I called after her. But she was too busy hurrying down the sidewalk to hear me.

CHAPTER 8

Most weekday nights Mary Fran deserted Christina and me as she left for the Kiwanis Center. Some evenings she went for math tutoring or the cooking class. But regardless of what the night offered, it seemed to be the whole evening that she looked forward to.

It seemed so special to her to be the busy person, to see Christina sitting on the floor working on the quilt she was making, and me sitting in the corner reading a book. We sat passively while she grabbed a number 17 bus schedule, reached for her raincoat, and called good-bye as she pulled the door closed behind her. Depending upon what the day had been like she would take off down the sidewalk with either confidence or relief, heading for the comfortingly familiar bus stop.

One Tuesday night towards the end of October, Mary Fran was upstairs getting ready to leave for the Kiwanis Center. I told Christina I was going along, too.

"It'll be on Tuesday and Thursday nights," I told her.

"What will be?" she asked absentmindedly as she cut triangles out of the fabric for her quilt.

"The Citizen Advocacy class I'm going to. Remember I told you I was going to become an advocate for someone, but first I had to go to a class?"

"No, I don't remember," Christina answered looking up from the material. "It's hard to keep everything straight when you get that glint in your eye and start talking in abbreviations." She pushed a strand of hair behind her ear and said with mock seriousness, " 'I'm going to O.V.R., and then maybe B.D.D., and probably W.A.R.C. But I've got C.A. tonight.' "

Looking at my reflection in the window I straightened my scarf and reached for my rain parka as I answered, "O.V.R.–Office of Vocational Rehabilitation, B.D.D.–Bureau of Developmental Disabilities, W.A.R.C.–Washington State Association for Retarded Citizens, C.A.–what does C.A. stand for?"

"Citizen Advocacy," Christina answered. "That's where you're going tonight."

"It's not abbreviated," I told her. "It's sort of like the Big Brothers/Big Sisters program. An Advocate is paired up with someone with a disability, they call that person your protégé. And what you do depends on what the person's special needs are. You might become involved in all sorts of legal problems, or you may just do recreational things together, or . . . "

I saw that Christina was looking down at her material again. It probably did seem like too much straining to her. But how could she know what it was like. Her parents had had four blue-eyed, blond-haired kids whose first conflict seemed to come their senior year of high school when they had to choose between Carleton College and the University of Chicago. Their idea of a family trauma was her brother's declaration that he wasn't going to take a fourth year of Latin.

So what's wrong with that? It's not very different from the way my family seemed in the family scrapbook, before Mary Fran and I were born. Like Christina's, our family seemed to be a family so healthy and happy and full of hope, the kind that turns away with polite discretion when they see a wheelchair or hear a stutter.

I watched Christina bend over as she cut the black velvet into a series of perfectly shaped circles. I wanted to say something else. We hadn't talked in weeks. I wanted to say something funny, to let her know I knew there was more than abbreviations and earnest advocate work. Not to be able to find Fran a job, to fail as an employment counselor, was one thing. But I even seemed to be failing as a roommate. Two years of college should have at least taught me how to be a compatible roommate.

"The thing about Citizen Advocacy is that it gives me a chance to give back. You know what I mean? We're getting so much from Seattle and the Kiwanis Center, and this gives me a chance to give a little back."

Christina nodded noncommittally as she continued to cut.

"Also, I really want Fran to get an advocate, but there's a waiting list. So, I thought if I could talk to the coordinator of the program . . . and since I'm volunteering myself . . . "

Christina smiled as she looked up, relieved to hear me scheming instead of propagandizing. "Seriously," she said, "I admire what you're doing."

"Ecch, I don't want to be admired," I answered, "I want to be lusted after."

Christina pushed her glasses up on her nose and frowned, "Which reminds me of that guy who's the head counselor at the Kiwanis Center, the happily married, middle-aged fellow."

"John Cozzolino," I sighed.

"For a future psychologist you're pretty dense," Christina laughed. "The only reason you have a crush on him is because he was the first person who was nice to you when you guys moved here! I hope you don't act silly around him."

"Of course not," I answered. "You don't give me much credit. When I see him I simply say 'Hi, John . . . then I swiftly genuflect and kiss his left shoe.'

"Anyway," I continued, "Go ahead and make fun of me, but I think he feels the same way about me."

"Oh, come on!" Christina said.

"Really . . . last week when I was at the Kiwanis Center signing up for Citizens Advocacy he came out of his office, and he put his hand on my shoulder and . . . ready for this . . . he looked deeply into my eyes and said, 'Hi, kiddo, how you doing?' "

"Sounds more like a coach talking to a football player," she said. "Is that all that happened?"

"Of course not," I answered. "Then I said, 'Fine, how are you?' Let's see, then what happened . . . it all happened so fast!"

"Yes," agreed Christina, "No time was wasted."

"It's important that I get the order right," I said, "Oh, now I remember . . . then he walked over to the front desk, picked up his mail, and walked back to his office."

Christina turned to Mary Fran who stood in the doorway buttoning her coat. "Take care of your little sister, Fran. She's in another weird mood; make sure she gets home safely tonight."

The two of them laughed, and Christina walked with us to the door where she turned on the porch light.

When we got to the Kiwanis Center Mary Fran went straight for the coat rack. I told her my meeting was upstairs. "I'll meet you down here afterwards," I started to add. But Mary Fran was already heading for the back room. This was her territory and she wasn't going to waste time chatting with me. I climbed the stairs to the top floor where there were two bathrooms, a kitchen, and a conference room. No one was in the conference room, but the light was on and there was a pile of papers and books on the table.

I sat down and waited, wondering what kind of people my classmates would be. Andrea Wilson, the Citizen Advocacy Coordinator, bustled in the doorway. When I had met her the week before she had told me that she recently moved with her children to Seattle from Los Angeles. She was divorced and her experience was in business and public relations.

She placed the film projector on the table next to the books. Just as I was ready to introduce myself—I'm Maureen Lynch, I was in last week and signed up for your program—Andrea finished counting the books and looked up. The distracted look of a harried organizer was promptly replaced with the warm smile of a long lost friend.

"Maureen! So glad you could make it. And Mary Jane, is she downstairs?"

I started to laugh and then decided that it would be easier for both of us if I didn't. "Oh, yeah, Mary Fran comes almost every night," I answered.

"Well, good for her," she said. Then her eyes glazed over as she turned away from me to count the chairs in the room and the styrofoam coffee cups in the corner. I wondered if I had looked that possessed when I organized Special Olympic meets and summer camp programs. It didn't take me long to realize that I had.

"Do you need any help?" I asked.

"Well, I was just thinking, could you run downstairs and get an extension cord? I think we're going to need it for the projector," Andrea said as she sat down at the table. "And let me think if there's anything else, while you're down there . . . " She took off her yellow and white polka-dotted blazer and folded it neatly over a chair. "No. No, I guess that's all for now," she decided.

Downstairs I looked for Pat, the Acitivites Director, who was leading everyone in a folk dance. When the tune finished she walked over to change the record. Everyone else dropped hands as they broke from the circle to talk and laugh and repeat certain steps they had had trouble with the first time. My eyes wandered through the group until I found Mary Fran. She was standing with some people who were listening to a fellow tell a story. I followed Mary Fran's face as she listened. At the puch line she moved her head to the left and laughed, and I smiled along mirroring her reaction.

Then I heard Pat's voice ask, "Can I help you?" I looked over at her and saw that she was talking to me. She didn't remember me and was wondering what I was doing, standing there watching so intently.

"Oh, yeah . . . um, I'm Mary Fran's sister. And I'm at a meeting upstairs. Andrea wanted me to get an extension cord," I stammered.

"Okay. Glen, will you help me out?" Pat called as she reached for another record. "Will you show her where we keep the extension cords?"

Glen, a young man who had stepped out from the group of folk dancers, directed me to a back closet. Digging around in a box on the bottom shelf he said, "Here, this is an extension cord."

Back upstairs I saw that four other people had come. They sat around the table quietly talking as Andrea stood in front threading the projector. I hoped I had missed the introductions—what your name is, what you do, and why you're there.

What was I—I wasn't a student, I wasn't really a teacher. Could you be a housewife and not be married? Men who stayed home and took care of household responsibilities called themselves "househusbands." Maybe I could be a "housesister." I decided to say I was a student; maybe I'd make up a new major.

Andrea began the meeting by writing her name on the blackboard; she was the regional coordinator for Citizen Advocacy, she explained. Then she mentioned her daughter, who was in classes for the learning disabled. Her talk, like herself, was a combination of troubled parent and savvy rhetorician, usually more of the latter. She turned to the young woman next to her and suggested, "Why don't you tell us about yourself?"

Becky, the young woman who was a sociology student at the University of Washington, defined herself with the adeptness of a current college student familiar with the trend of beginning classes that way. There was another University of Washington student, a housewife, and a young man who was an accountant.

After seeing a movie, *Something Shared,* about an advocate and a protégée, Andrea passed out a booklet to each of us. She told us that it was important that we try to understand the current prejudices facing people who are mentally retarded. At the word "prejudice," the housewife looked concerned and the accountant seemed worried. The two college students seemed determined to oblige. Andrea stood up and moved to the blackboard.

"I think you'll understand what I mean if we just start listing some. Some biases are old wives' tales, and some, I think you'll be surprised to find, are still very much alive, and well, and living in you. Let's just start throwing some out . . . give me some attitudes toward mentally retarded people."

No one said anything. Andrea looked around at us, and her eyes settled on my face with the uncomfortable look of a teacher asking to be bailed out.

"I guess one is the idea of a mentally retarded person as a child," I answered. "You know, the 'eternal child' who is always smiling and happy and doesn't know any better. We sort of push this image ourselves, though, by showing only pictures of cute and cuddly little kids when we do fund-raising."

Andrea looked relieved. She turned to the blackboard and wrote a large number one–"The Eternal Child, never feels pain or disappointment." "Very good, Maureen!" she said.

Becky, one of the college students, raised her hand and said, "Going along with the concept of the sole image we show being that of a child . . . telethons and other fund-raising events exploit the public's pity by presenting a handicapped person as helpless, always the recipient of aid. You seldom see pictures of people who have jobs or who are active members of the community."

"Very important point, Becky! Any feedback?" Andrea asked.

Ethel, the woman who had said she was a housewife, softly answered, "That's true, we're taught to think of all retarded people as helpless. But it's strange that parents are told it's okay to institutionalize a retarded child. I mean, if you have a normal child you wouldn't dare think of giving him up. But you have a retarded child, who everyone thinks is helpless, and suddenly it's okay, it's almost like it's expected of you."

I wondered what was behind her words. Ethel had said it so movingly, she was almost in tears. At class the next week I'd find out. She would take me aside and tell me about the call she had gotten from a social worker at Pine Grove State Hospital. The woman wanted Ethel to visit her brother because he was being considered for "placement in the community." Many of the buildings at the institution were being closed, the social worker explained, and the people were being moved to small group homes in various neighborhoods so they could live a more normal life.

Ethel's memories of her brother had blurred through the years. Her parents were dead, and she hadn't even told her husband about him. He just didn't seem real to her. She tried to pull together the memories. All she could remember was her mother taking presents to him, returning with tears staining her face, the shopping bag empty and her eyes puffy.

He was five years older than Ethel and had never lived at home. The only one who visited him was her mother. So through the years he had remained faceless. Sometimes she would overhear her parents talking about him. He was named David, after her father. But they seldom used his name. Faceless and nameless.

"And now I'm supposed to care," Ethel said to me. I started to say something. I didn't know what to say but I wanted to make her stop. "I suppose you think I'm terrible," she said twirling the coffee that was in the bottom of her styrofoam cup. Our class had taken a break, and we were all headed downstairs to get sodas from the machine. As I was on my way out Ethel had called to me.

Now she sat at a table across from me. "I suppose you think I'm terrible. But I thought maybe you could help me. . . . Andrea told us about you and your sister Mary Jane," she explained.

"Mary Fran," I corrected.

"Oh, sorry, she said Mary Jane. Anyway, that first night, you know, when you went downstairs for the extension cord. She told us about how you're giving up a year of college to live with your sister."

Oh, God, I could imagine Andrea talking about us, glibly exploiting our gut aches with the slickness of an advertising executive. What were we, the basis for her new campaign? Join Citizen Advocacy and you'll meet the Lynch gals, they look alike, they move alike, they're only fifteen months apart in age, *but* . . . .

I stood up to get some coffee. I hate coffee, but I needed to turn away from her. She had thrown it all out so quickly, and it lay there throbbing vulnerably on the table between us.

"Ethel, I don't . . ."

"I've got five kids, three are still at home. What am I supposed to do, bring home this stranger and say 'Meet your Uncle Davey?' Listen, Maureen, I just want to ask you one thing. The next time they call . . . from the institution . . . will you go with me to see him? I don't know what to expect, I've never even seen a picture of him."

I took a deep breath and looked past her out the window. The Space Needle was lit up with a red light on top. Becky walked in with a can of 7-Up.

"Un-do it, un-do it, drink 7-Up," she sang happily. Then she turned to us with a wide smile and said, "Two more classes, ladies! And we will be entering the great beyond to join the ranks of the advocates who have gone before us."

Tom, the accountant, who was walking in the door behind her laughed, "I think what you're suffering from is more midterm hysteria, Becky. But I toast your sentiments!" They

clanked soda cans and then began to talk about the ridiculously high price the soda machine had demanded.

"Will you, Maureen?" Ethel repeated. "Will you go with
me?"

Reaching into my purse I found a piece of paper and said,
"Yeah . . . I will, Ethel. Here's my phone number."

CHAPTER 9

One afternoon Evelyn Greer parked her pickup truck with the camper in back in front of our house. She got out and pulled her navy blue parka down around her hips. Then she brushed her gray-black bangs out of her face as she looked up at our house. Evelyn, who was a wonderful combination of Margaret Mead and Girl Scout troop leader, was Mary Fran's Citizen Advocate.

We had spoken briefly on the phone before. And, as she stood on our front porch, she seemed to be viewing the whole scene as slightly ludicrous. I welcomed her inside trying to be a perfect host. I offered her some zucchini bread Mary Fran and I had made the day before. Evelyn accepted the bread and peppermint tea and sat down on the couch.

She explained that she had joined Citizen Advocacy at her daughter's urging. Evelyn had retired from teaching, then when her husband died, she decided to move from their Montana home to the city–Seattle. She took a sip of tea and laughed, "Actually I'm enjoying my retirement very much. But Sarah convinced me I needed to be doing more. My daughter's a psychiatric nurse," she added fondly, "And sometimes she just gets carried away with her diagnoses."

Mary Fran sat quietly on the couch watching Evelyn with quick, sideways glances.

"Montana is one of my favorite places," I said.

"Really?" asked Evelyn incredulously, "Why?"

"It seems to have everything," I answered. "Mountains, lakes, and real snow in the winter, not like Seattle."

"It certainly does have snow," she agreed. "And when you're snowed in, miles and miles from anyone else, snow's about the only thing it does have . . . no, I think I prefer Seattle." She looked over at Mary Fran and asked, "Where do your parents live?"

Mary Fran looked at me, then back at Evelyn. "Michigan," she answered.

"Our mother lives in Michigan," I said. "Our father died when we were little. He died of a heart attack . . . about eleven years ago."

"Your mother never remarried?" Evelyn asked.

"No," I answered. "After Dad died we moved to South Haven, a place we used to just live in the summer. And Fran and I went to school there . . . most of Mom's relatives live there. But now that we're both done with school she wants to sell the house and move."

"Where to?" Evelyn asked.

"She's not sure," I said. "But she keeps saying 'someplace warm.' "

"Well, enough of this talking," Evelyn said as she finished her tea and put the ceramic mug down. "Would you like to go for a ride, Mary?"

"Yes," Mary Fran answered, glad that she wouldn't have to share her friend with me.

Evelyn turned to me and said, "I think we'll go down along the marina to Golden Gardens Parks. So we'll see you in . . . well, we'll just see you when we get back!" Evelyn turned to smile smugly at Mary Fran as if they were scheming to run away from home. Mary Fran laughed as she followed her out to the truck.

I took the dishes into the kitchen and was rinsing them when the phone rang. "Quick, tell me what you were just doing," the voice demanded. It was Patricia, our sister, calling from New York.

"I was in the kitchen washing dishes . . . and gazing at the waxy build-up on my floor," I answered.

"Disgusting!" Patricia said. "You're really going to go into shock when you leave your domestic tranquility to come back here for school."

"If you'd like a taste of 'domestic tranquility' we could trade for a month," I said. Afterwards I wished I hadn't said that. But we couldn't spend the rest of our lives cautiously weighing our words because of what had happened two months before.

In August when I had been home in Michigan, I had thought at first that it would just be for two weeks. Then I was planning to leave for New York to finish college. Everything seemed perfect. I had transferred from Carleton College to the New School for Social Research, and I was excited about the prospect of living in New York. The two summers of going to school were about to pay off—I would be finishing college the following spring, in just three years.

But at home I had found myself face-to-face with Mary Fran's frustrations. It hadn't seemed as bad in Mom's letters. Maybe she didn't write much about it. Or maybe I was too busy to notice the frantic tone. Too busy counting credits, and pulling my own version of Mary Fran's tantrums which ended up leading to my decision to transfer. But it wasn't that easy for Mary Fran. She couldn't just pick up a catalogue and decide to transfer to another school.

After I had decided to live with her for a year, I began to reconsider. It wasn't a wholehearted turnaround. But maybe, I began to imagine, I could help her and still go to school. We could both go to New York, I suggested to Mom, and

I'd just take one or two classes then work with Mary Fran the rest of the time.

"It just might work," Mom had said hopefully, "Call Patricia and see what she thinks."

"She'll probably love the idea," I said as I dialed her number. "Their apartment is huge and we'd be two more people to split the rent."

"Oh, God, Mo! I don't want her here," Patricia had answered.

I don't remember what else we said, it wasn't much. I tried to hold the phone so she couldn't hear my crying. And I heard her trying to regain control of her voice. Her answer had shot out at me, the tone so cold and furious, the words bitter.

I swallowed and moved the phone down to my mouth. "Look, let's just hang up, okay?" I said. "It was probably a bad idea anyway. Call in a couple of days and we'll straighten it all out. It's no big thing."

When I hung up I looked over at Mom. She had followed the whole conversation with a worried look. Her eyes looked troubled and she seemed ready to cry herself. I walked into the living room and sat down. Mom had followed and sat across from me on the couch.

I had never felt so alone and scared as I had that last week in August. Everyone seemed so distant, and at the same time they seemed to be turning to me, expecting me to have answers to Mary Fran's troubles. Why me, I had felt like asking, I'm the baby of the family, remember?

Mary Fran was camping in Seattle with Philip then. Mom was leaving the next day to pick her up. She had hoped she could arrive with the message that they'd be back next month—if Mary Fran agrees, Mo's going to take the year off from school. But it all seemed to be crumbling.

I had sat across from Mom pushing the words at her. I was determined to convince myself that Patricia was right, she had the guts to say what she felt, she must be right. Big sisters are always right. She was six years older than I and

I had idolized everything about her. Patricia had always seemed so grown-up . . . so funny . . . so special. In the plays that our children's theatre group had put on I was always in the middle of the mob of elves or fairies or munchkins. But she had always had big parts, parts with words. Everything about her seemed so important.

Now, two months later, she was talking to me on the phone telling me funny stories about acting auditions she had gone to, and how much she hated her waitressing job. I made jokes about the rain in Seattle, and described our house. We hung up satisfied that things were okay between us . . . that it really wasn't any big thing.

I went into the living room and sat down. Mary Fran and Evelyn would probably be home soon. But it was nice to be alone for a while. I thought about that last week in August. I hadn't been able to convince myself that Patricia was right. Mom had gone into the kitchen to make us tea. And I sat there alone, sobbing loudly, tears running down my face, my nose running, and my chest pounding. She had come back and handed me a cup of tea.

I wiped my face with a tissue and said between sobs, "I don't know if I can do it."

"You don't have to," Mom answered.

I didn't believe that. Anyway it wasn't the point. I knew we were going to try.

"You've always been strong," Mom told me. "When you were little, people thought you two were twins because you were so close in age. You used to teach her things, and you two would make up games . . . in school Patricia described your adventures to everyone—'Mary Fran and Mo stories' she called them—the kids loved them. But you were always the leader of the two. I remember your father was so surprised when he'd tell you to do something, and you wouldn't pay any attention to him."

The memory I had of my father was that his authority went unquestioned. He was a man who had tried to share his life with us by occasionally dragging us to Notre Dame football games. The rest of the time he seemed to be waiting for us to finish being kids and grow up.

"You mean I ignored him?" I asked.

"Oh, no, you'd listen," Mom answered. But you always made up your own mind. And George was always amazed that such a young child could be so independent."

One of the memories I have of him is when he taught me how to tell time. I had come home from school sure I would never be able to learn that. When our teacher had held up the homemade clock, I had become so confused. What did a paper plate have to do with telling time? It seemed so easy to everyone else. So I had just sat there thinking I'll never be able to learn, I'll never be able to learn. When I later repeated my decision that I would never be able to tell time, Dad had said, "That's ridiculous! Come here, Mo." He took his watch off his wrist and it became a debate of wills. While he simply outlined the basics, I kept repeating my mantra: "I won't be able to learn, I won't be able to!" But there was no paper plate and no yarn or construction paper decorations. What he was saying was so clear. My words stopped and all that came out of my mouth was, "Oh!" When he heard that, he put the watch back on his wrist and went back to reading the evening paper.

I seldom thought of my father without remembering that Saturday morning he died. Mom had woken me up by leaning over my bed and saying, "Maureen! Wake up, your father's dead!" I remember her panicky face as she turned to the only other person home, her ten-year-old daughter.

He had been pretty independent-minded himself, having a heart attack in the middle of the night without even telling us. He died in February. He could have at least waited until a holiday when Philip or Patricia would have been home from school. They both went away to high school, boarding schools out of state. I was too young to know what to do, how to help Mom.

I wish I had known my father better. He seems so distant. And so I continue to make up memories about him that he didn't have time to live. I remember him talking to Philip and Patricia about going away to high school. He felt it was an advantage he had missed. He must have been confused by their tears. He thought it was a wonderful gift.

When I was fourteen Mom gave me a choice—St. Mary's Academy in South Bend where Patricia had gone, or South Haven Public High School. The decision was easy. I stayed home. I'd like to think he'd agree with my choices, be proud of my successes. But I don't really know. I wonder if I'm still in fourth grade to him. Still frozen in his mind, like a scene from a movie when the projector is stopped.

I had never thought about my Dad and his feelings about Mary Fran. But then Mom told me that the only time she ever saw him cry was when they returned home from dropping Fran off at Our Lady of Providence that first time. It was late at night, and we were all worn by the long drive and the echoes of Mary Fran's screams not to leave her. Philip, Patricia, and I were all upstairs in our own bedrooms trying to push the day out of our heads. Mom and Dad sat downstairs in the kitchen with their drinks.

My father was an active, robust man who seemed capable of managing almost anything. Words came easily to him, whether he was telling a story to friends at a party or presenting a case in court. But that night when he wiped away the tears of helplessness that ran down his face, he was reduced to clichés. "My God," he said to Mom. "She depends on us so much. What's going to happen to her when we die?"

I tried to think about what it was like from his viewpoint. It comes out like a modern fable, but I'm not sure what the moral of the story is. It couldn't have been very easy for him though. My father was used to being a winner. Like any Irish Catholic boy who went to Notre Dame he must have thought he was well on his way. He made the football team. And he wore his letter sweater home on the holidays. He stayed at Notre Dame for his law degree. Then he returned to his hometown. He was in no hurry to marry until he met a young nurse who was also in no hurry to marry. They married immediately.

Their first child was a boy. Four years later they had a girl. His private law practice was going well. Four years later another child was expected. This time they didn't care whether it was a boy or a girl "as long as it was healthy."

It was a girl. And she wasn't healthy. Her development was slow. A year and a half later there was an unexpected birth—another girl. But the main concern had become the third born. She was beginning to crawl, and it had become obvious that she was developing slower.

Mary Fran's problems became a part of the baggage that we carried with us to restaurants and on trips. It was so obvious that complete strangers at adjoining tables would discuss her difference. Our difference. It must have been quite a shock to a nurse and a lawyer, people who had careers built on giving advice to others. The tables had been suddenly turned on them.

Mom sat across from me watching me closely. She seemed embarrassed when she saw me look up at her. Looking away quickly she said quietly, "You never really seemed like the youngest." Then she left to pack. Her flight for Seattle was the next afternoon.

The next day, after I returned from driving Mom to the airport, both Philip and Patricia called. "I've been thinking about it," Patricia told me, her voice aloof and flat. "And I'll live with you, but not here," she added. "The only reason I'm here is because of acting. I hate New York. I'll help you with her, but somewhere else."

"No, we're going to live in Seattle," I answered. "I've got to feel Fran out about it when she gets back. But it sounds like it would be the perfect place. Philip called today and . . . " My voice was over-animated as I described Seattle's assets.

Before hanging up I assured her, "It's just a matter of timing. It's important for you to be auditioning now. You know that if I were doing something as important I wouldn't give it up, and it would probably be you planning this."

"You think so?" Patricia asked.

"Of course," I assured her.

I was tired of talking about it. Tired of making excuses for everyone. I didn't tell Patricia all that Philip had said. Philip had called because he said he had forgotten Mom's flight number. But he continued to talk. It took me a while to understand what he was trying to say.

"We have to face Mary Fran's problems," he told me.

"Of course," I answered.

It wasn't unusual, he continued. He had seen many mentally retarded people in the psychiatric clinic where he worked as a counselor.

"They often have problems facing the reality of their limitations," he insisted.

"What are you getting at?" I had finally asked.

"She's worse than I thought," he answered. "Frequent mood changes, very argumentative." He sounded like he was reading a textbook, not talking about his sister.

"You mean you're telling me we should put her in a psychiatric ward? Just throw some thorazine down her and she'll come to her senses?" I asked angrily.

"Mo, stop playing the irate heroine!" he said. "I just want you to know that it's pretty serious. And about institutionalizing her . . . well, we shouldn't rule out the possibility. We have to be realistic, and there just aren't that many choices."

His voice sounded so sensible and kind. It scared me because he was probably right. But he also sounded distant. I wondered if this was the voice he used for talking to his clients at the psychiatric clinic.

"There are very few alternatives," Philip continued. "I can't help her. The few days we've been back from camping she's had Betty all upset. She just sits and stares at her."

"Who wouldn't, your wife is fascinating," I said.

And for the first time all week I wished Patricia were home so we could join in sister-in-law jokes. The caricature we had drawn of our Southern, army base-raised sister-in-law bore little resemblance to the real person. But it didn't make indulging in the jokes any less fun.

"Oh, cut it out!" he said. His prediction began to seem less threatening. When his voice lost the sound of the sensible counselor, I realized that he was as confused as I was. He felt the pull of responsibility from his family and from Betty. I could take a year off from college. But you can't very easily put a wife on hold for a year.

My thoughts were brought back to the present by Christina's returning home.

"Good day, lady of leisure," she said as she walked into the living room. "What are you doing?"

"I was just thinking about this summer . . . about my family," I answered. "I'm waiting for Fran to get home. I thought we could go downtown and get some pumpkins."

"Good idea," she said. "I think we'd get kicked out of Ballard if we didn't celebrate Halloween like everyone else. Where's Fran?" I told her about Evelyn.

"What happened yesterday?" Christina asked. "You answered the ad at the rest home, didn't you? The Norse Home."

"Yeah, we went," I answered. "But nothing much happened. The director was a nice guy. He didn't know what to make of us at first. I think I'm getting paranoid, I get the feeling that everyone thinks we're crazy for even trying. Anyway, he said to call him next week. He didn't really promise us anything. But he said, in this heavy Norwegian accent, 'Don't you give up, your sister needs you so. Maybe we can work something out.' "

I looked up and laughed. But Christina looked distracted. And I realized that it was more than just roommate camaraderie that had prompted her to ask.

"Do you think Fran could do it?" Christina asked. "I mean if she got the job, do you really think she could do the work?"

"It's just a maid's job, Christina," I answered. "The responsibilities are to clean the floor, collect linen, things like that. Oh, I guess she'd need help in the beginning . . . remembering everything. But once she got it into a sequence she'd be great. I wish we'd finally get it settled. The past two months have really dragged . . . What's up?" I was beginning to hope that maybe Christina had come across something for Fran in her own job hunting. Why else would she suddenly be so interested in Fran's capability?

Christina continued to look out the window, "Well, I just wondered," she said slowly as she looked over at me. "I just wanted to know . . . would you mind if I went there for an interview?"

I would never have guessed she would ask that. She knew as well as I did that once she appeared for an interview any half-promises the director had made to us would be thrown out the window.

"Of course not," I answered. "It's up to you."

I was too surprised to say anything else. I couldn't believe Christina would do that to Mary Fran. I could see her discomfort that her attempt to find a job had come to this.

"Well, it's just that . . . I always . . yeah, I know it's up to me," she said as she walked away.

There seemed to be no way Mary Fran could win. Not only would Christina end up with the job, but the whole time she would feel as if she were slumming to have competed with Mary Fran in the first place.

The thing that hurt the most was knowing that I was more like Christina than I was like Mary Fran. People like Christina and I would always have alternatives, even if they were sometimes limited. But Mary Fran didn't seem to have any.

CHAPTER 10

Our Citizen Advocacy class ended. And we celebrated our graduation by finding out the name of our protégées while eating an ice cream cake Andrea had brought. My protégée was Laura, a nineteen-year-old who attended a local public school's special education class. One of my classmates, Tom, offered advice on what buses to take to get to her home in West Seattle. It would be a long trip from our neighborhood of Ballard. If I didn't make the right connections for express buses, it would take me over two hours. But that didn't seem important then.

We were all very excited. Becky knew sign language so she was paired with a little girl with a hearing impairment. Tom, the accountant, turned out to be a Seattle Supersonics fanatic. He hoped that the young man he was matched with would share his basketball enthusiasm. We laughed at our own excitement. And Ethel compared us to giggly school children with their first pen pals.

Before the evening was over Ethel told me that she'd call me so we could go to Pine Grove together to see "him." "My brother," she corrected herself. She told me it would probably be the end of next month, around Thanksgiving. She didn't say it with irony, she was probably mentally planning her family responsibilities so she could fit in time for him. The shopping . . . cooking . . . gathering of grown children home again for a holiday. Then, while everyone was distracted, a quick side trip to the institution. It was probably very much the way her own mother had planned her visits.

I wondered what we'd be doing on Thanksgiving. That was four weeks away. Anything could happen in four weeks. Fran could have a job, Christina could finish her quilt, Mom could have found someone to buy the house, Betty could have a baby . . . Well, maybe not in four weeks. My thoughts had begun to center on planning everyone else's lives. Then I remembered that my birthday was on Thanksgiving this year, I'd be twenty-one.

The next day I followed Tom's directions and took a bus downtown, then transferred to an express bus to West Seattle. It was a four-block walk from the bus stop to Laura's house. I kept looking at the piece of paper in my hand that had her address on it. The ink was smeared from the rain. It was really stupid of me to think that the sky would stay clear; my sneakers were soaked. I would probably drip all over Laura, and she'd want to trade me in for someone else.

The only thing I knew about Laura was that she was a senior in high school, and that she lived with her parents. She didn't have any brothers or sisters. I looked down at the paper in my hand and looked up at the mailbox in front of me. The addresses were the same so I rang the bell.

A short, frail woman who was probably Laura's mother answered the door. She wore dark glasses and a determinedly friendly mouth.

"You must be Maureen," she said. "Oh, how Laura's been looking forward to your coming!" She welcomed me into their living room. The drapes were drawn, and it was dark and stuffy. Small porcelain animals crowded on the shelves and table tops. She told me to relax and dry off while she went to get Laura.

"I'll be right back," Mrs. Barnes said. "Laura must be in her bedroom. We're so glad you're here." She left the small room through a nearby doorway, and I could hear her whispering in the other room. I looked around and saw a picture on top of the TV. It looked like a school picture. The young woman had long, straight brown hair, an easy, friendly smile, and big dark eyes. She had on a red turtleneck sweater. She didn't look at all like the tiny, straining woman who was her mother.

"Well, here we are," Mrs. Barnes announced. I turned from the picture to the doorway where the voice was. Mrs. Barnes was standing there with a tall, thin young woman whose eyes focused beyond me. She stood rigidly with her elbows bent and stuck to her waist. Her fists were clenched and stuck out in front of her. The mother nodded her head as she smiled hopefully at me. Then she nodded again and raised her eyebrows.

"Here we are," she repeated.

I realized that I had been missing my cues. "Hi, Laura," I said. "I'm Maureen."

Then I stood up and walked over to her where I smiled and put out my hand. Mrs. Barnes stood with her arm around Laura's waist, holding her tense body close. Her hand rested on Laura's locked elbow.

"Laura, Maureen wants to shake your hand," she said. Laura didn't move. Her eyes still focused beyond me. "Laura!" Mrs. Barnes said, but her eyes looked accusingly at me.

"That's all right," I said. "Let's sit down, we can get to know each other."

I zeroed in on the couch where I had left my sweater. Sitting down I clutched it in front of me. Mrs. Barnes sat on the other end of the couch. Laura walked stiffly to a small stool that was near the TV.

"That's Laura's school picture from last fall," Mrs. Barnes said brightly.

"I was just looking at it," I said. "It's a nice picture. I'm a real camera buff. . . . " My mouth seemed to have been taken over by some stranger. I heard myself make a feeble joke about how everyone in my family gets mad at me for following them around and taking pictures. But I felt like I had to say something. It was painful to see the picture Laura and the real Laura together. The relaxed, smiling Laura in the picture seemed to mock the tense, troubled Laura who crouched on a stool below it.

"Of course that was before Laura had her little problem," Mrs. Barnes said. "But she's getting better, much better than when she was in the hospital. She'll probably be going back to school soon. Won't that be nice?"

"Yes, it really will!" I said. I listened in disbelief to my voice as it left my mouth.

"Not that it hasn't been nice having her home," she said. "I have a vision problem and Laura is wonderful to have as a helper . . . in the kitchen . . . dusting. But the people in the hospital said she should get back to school as soon as possible."

"Laura, do you like to cook?" I asked.

Slowly her eyes moved to my face. "I just wondered if you like to cook," I repeated. "I thought we could cook something together sometime. Maybe some bread . . . I really like to make bread from scratch. Do you like to cook?"

"Yes, I do," she answered, her voice sounding like it was a record on the wrong speed.

"She certainly does," Mrs. Barnes said. "I think that was one of the things she missed most when she was in the hospital—not being able to help me in the kitchen."

"What hospital were you in?" I asked looking at Laura.

"Harborview Medical Center," Mrs. Barnes answered.

"My brother works there," I said.

"How nice," she answered.

"Well, I should get home," I said. "Now I know how to get

here. Um, I'll call you next week Laura, and we can decide what we want to do."

"That will be very nice," Mrs. Barnes said as she showed me to the door.

Waiting at the bus stop I tried to remember what Andrea had told me about Laura. The bus to downtown splattered its way to the curb. And I got in the nearly empty bus. It was six o'clock and everyone else was going in the opposite direction. I must have forgotten something Andrea told me. She didn't describe Laura at all like she was. But she really hadn't described her.

Andrea had told me that Laura had always been in special education classes, that she would be graduating soon, and that she had some emotional problems as a result of finishing school. Laura's mother remembered the day that Laura had stopped eating, and began to walk with stiff joints and a fixed gaze. It had happened soon after the summer day that she got a letter from her school listing graduation requirements. "Too much pressure," Mrs. Barnes had sighed. On the ride home I stared out the window at the darkening sky. I wondered how Fran was.

When I got home the house was empty. Fran was at the Kiwanis Center, taking part in the Wednesday Night Supper Club. And Christina wasn't home from her job at the Norse Home yet. I reached for the phone to call Mom.

"I'm glad you called," Mom said. "I wanted to tell you something that happened today." Then she told me about seeing one of Fran's old teachers at the post office. The teacher had asked how she was, Mom said with unbridled smugness. "And I told her that she was living in Seattle with you, and that she had learned how to bus downtown and back all by herself."

Most of the teachers at Mary Fran's old school were sure that Mary Fran would soon be back, that there was little else for her. Mom was bristling with energy as she repeated the story to me.

Mom changed her voice as she repeated the teacher's

words. " 'Busing alone? Why that's strange, isn't it? She never did that when she lived here with you!' I thought, why you silly fool, you'll never give in, will you! South Haven doesn't even have any buses. But she had to get in one last dig that I was a bad parent."

"Did you say anything?" I asked.

"Not really," Mom answered. "She was determined to get the last word in. Before she left she said, 'Tillie, what do you think this is going to prove? So Mo works with her for a year. And she learns how to bus alone, maybe even how to buy groceries, a few other things. Then what happens to her? She won't fit in aywhere! There's no going back now, you know.' "

"At first I just laughed at her," Mom continued. "I thought she just didn't like being proven wrong. But she's right. After the way she's living this year—like any other young woman who's trying to make it on her own—there's no way she could go back to riding a school bus with little kids, and to a job of sanding wood in a sheltered workshop. Of course she won't have to. We're going to find something better. But it's a frightening thought, that you have to limit people just so they'll fit into the few existing programs. I don't really . . . "

"Mom," I interrupted, "Mom, we're coming home."

"What?" she asked. "What do you mean? For Thanksgiving?"

"No, for good," I answered letting out a sigh of relief. "It's just not working out."

"I don't understand," she said. "I thought everything was going so well. What happened?"

"Oh, it's going just great!" I said sarcastically. "Couldn't be better, why, she's learned how to bus—wonder of wonders! Who could have predicted that would happen after three trips every day for seven weeks, twenty-one hours a week of drilling on the change needed and where to get off: 'A nickel and a quarter, the red house on the corner, a nickel and a quarter, the red house on the corner!' "

"You're not being fair, Maureen," Mom said. "She bused

to Philip and Betty's. And you hadn't taken the bus there many times."

"Sure she got there," I agreed. "But it took her two hours longer than it should have. I still don't know where she was. But Betty called me every fifteen mintues. And Philip was driving aound the neighborhood, trying to find her without her seeing him. He finally went home. We were just about to call the police when she rang their doorbell."

"I didn't know that," Mom said quietly.

"We didn't want to worry you," I said. "A lot of other things have happened. And now each time she's late, or isn't home, or something's wrong I begin to hope it's serious, so that we can finally give up. So that we can stop trying . . . finally stop hoping. God, Mom, don't you know what I mean? Have you ever felt this way?"

"Of course I've felt that way!" she said angrily. "All those years, those smug diagnoses . . . one of the first times I thought we might be able to help her was when I read about a clinic in Philadelphia that had developed something new, something they called patterning. She was only four, it might have helped her. Maybe not. But George said I was being ridiculous, that I couldn't go flying out east when we had three other children."

"Yeah, I've read about that clinic," I said. "But what were you going to do with me? If Fran was only four, I was two-and-a-half."

"I didn't really think about you," she said. "Anymore than I thought about Patricia or Philip. I just knew that she needed special help. I thought maybe they could give it."

"But what do you think now?" I asked. "What makes you keep trying, what makes you so sure that more is what's best for her?"

"I keep trying," she said gently, "because it's all we can do."

"I don't know," I said. "I don't know, Mom. Today I saw somebody, a young girl who's nineteen. She just had one more year of school to go, and she'd have had her high school diploma. She just went along, following what everyone thought was best for her. And then one day before her senior year she clammed up. She crawled inside of herself. They had to take her to the hospital where Philip works and feed her intravenously. I met her today. There's no way you could put demands on her now. She's like a zombie."

"But she's different from someone like Mary Fran," Mom said. "No one's forcing her, Mary Fran's the one who wants more."

"That's what I'm not sure about," I said. "You should have seen her when they told her she wouldn't work out at that day care center, Happy Faces. She was relieved, it was too much for her. Sometimes I think everything is, that she'd be just as happy following me around."

"Where is she now?" Mom asked. "I don't want her to hear us talking like this."

"At the Kiwanis Center," I answered.

"Maybe she's just not showing her disappointment," Mom said. "You're still approaching each job with hope, and then feeling crushed when it falls through. Maybe she's at the point where she can't let herself get as involved."

"I hope you're right," I said. "Because if she has a breakdown it would be too much for me to handle. I'd probably have one, too. Then you'd have two of us on your hands."

"Philip would take care of you," she answered.

"Thanks a lot," I said. "Wouldn't you even come to visit?"

"Only on alternate Wednesdays," she answered. "We better hang up, you're going to have a horrible phone bill."

"Okay," I said. "I'll call you next week."

Our phone bill was horrible that year. But I continued to depend on Mom for encouraging words. Just knowing that someone else knew, that I could talk to someone without having to keep on an optimistic front helped. The times before the holidays were the worst. Nothing was given, we had to put together everything from leisure time, to work, to a schedule of household chores. But the thing that was hardest was the frightening feeling that we would have to make it, because there was nothing to go home to.

CHAPTER 11

Mary Fran was in a two-week workshop at the Kiwanis Center. It was held every day from one to four. Led by a young therapist, it was designed to give the fifteen people a chance to "talk about their concerns and begin to determine their priorities."

The therapist who was leading the group was a young woman in her thirites with long, streaked hair and aviator-frame glasses. "It's sort of a combination assertiveness training and goal clarification," she told me. Mary Fran was interested in the chance to hear other people talk about their lives, their problems, their dreams. She was also glad for the chance to get away from me.

I was her only teacher as we worked on the daily lessons—independent living skills, community awareness skills, job-readiness skills . . . A mutiny would soon be in the works if we didn't come up with some variety. While looking through the neighborhood newspaper I found an interesting ad in the classified section offering tutoring.

Maybe this would be a good time to try a tutor to teach

Fran reading. She had never been given reading lessons. We had always hoped that she might be able to learn to read . . . someday. But at the same time I felt sort of silly for wanting to ask. After all, no one had ever tried to teach her. That must mean something.

It's a strange thing, but when parents of children who have cerebral palsy, a hearing impairment, or some other physical handicap are told of their child's disability, they often ask, "But he isn't mentally retarded . . . is he?" Because to them the term quite simply means "unable to learn." I guess mental retardation is thought of as the bottom of the barrel.

Parents who have a mentally retarded child, however, often jump years into the future. And, as if they are trying to get a handle on what that ominous term means, on just exactly how it will shape their child's life, they often ask, "Will he ever learn to read?" To a mentally retarded person, and his family, reading seems to separate the men from the boys, or the "Low Level" from the "Capable."

Many mentally retarded people who are in their twenties and older have never been exposed to reading lessons. In many schools it was just assumed it would be a waste of time. As attitudes and pedagogic thought have changed, some people have begun to try tutors. Other people will never have the chance to learn.

A common approach now being used is to teach a memorized vocabulary of words, sight words, that can be used frequently during the day. The emphasis is on the practical. They would be words like a person's name, so he could eventually use a time clock at work. And other words like "stop" and "walk" for traffic lights, and "women" and "men" for bathroom doors.

Once when a college teacher heard I had a sister who couldn't read, she said in class, "Here's a perfect example." Walking to the blackboard she had her chalk poised and asked, "Now what sight words would you like your sister to learn?"

"I don't want her to learn sight words," I had answered. "I want her to learn to read."

I want to be able to write letters to her, and have her read them and write back. I want her to be able to go into the library and take books out. Not like now when she has to sit on the low benches in the little kid section and look at picture books. Or has to wait until we have the time to read to her. Why should I assume she can't read just because she's never had the chance?

I'm afraid my teacher was disappointed. She was expecting a reasonable answer. She had wanted me to parrot out, "stop, walk, women, men, danger, exit, restaurant." But the subject of reading is a loaded topic. As unreasonable as we may know it is, we still feel that reading would be a shield for the person we're concerned about; their protection against being exploited, laughed at, mugged . . . it would make them less different. And it would be proof of their worth.

So many times teachers find our requests unreasonable. And they wonder why we keep dwelling on reading. They wonder why we can't just appreciate what is being taught. If only they could understand. It's not that we disagree with their teaching priorities. And it's often not even that we really feel reading is that important. It's not so much that we want to introduce them to Proust as it is that we want to protect them from the neighborhood bullies.

"Listen to this, Fran," I said. "Someone put an ad in the paper, 'Will tutor. Children or adults. M.A. in Special Education. Sheila. 783-8704.' "

"For me?" she asked.

"Yeah, that's what I was thinking," I said. "We'd have to find out how much she charges. But you and I could keep working on using the laundromat, buying groceries, the kinds of things we do around here. And you have Mrs. Sanders at the Kiwanis Center for math tutoring every Monday night. Maybe a third person would be good. We'd have to . . ."

"Call her," Mary Fran interrupted. We walked to the phone

together, and I dialed as Mary Fran stood beside me and smiled.

I told the voice that answered what my name was and that we had seen her ad. "She wants to know," I said aside to Fran, "if we can meet her this afternoon."

"No," Mary Fran said as if she were an executive talking to her secretary. "No way, have class at Kiwanis Center."

"I forgot," I said into the phone, "My sister's in a workshop that's meeting the rest of this week."

"You go," Mary Fran whispered. "You go, Mo. Can tell me later what she like."

At the same time Sheila was suggesting, "Well then, why don't the two of us meet and you can describe what your sister's like, and what her special needs are."

"Fine," I said. "Since Mary Fran is so busy maybe it would be best for the two of us to meet." Mary Fran beamed and Sheila agreed. Sheila gave me the name of a restaurant to meet her at. It was in Pioneer Square, the newly renovated area downtown that was full of wrought iron lamp posts, tiny restaurants, and shops full of imported clothing. She has expensive taste, I thought, as I went upstairs to borrow the blazer from Christina's interview outfit.

That afternoon I sat in an indoor court that was designed to look like an old-fashioned ice-cream parlor. Pioneer Square was the oldest part of the city. It had become quite a popular place. But the old standbys who had known it during its less-affluent time couldn't be persuaded to leave. They stayed on, drinking Thunderbird out of paper bags. The row of men leaned over their crossed legs talking to their paper bags. Sharing the same bench were two middle-aged women whose clothes and accessories were stamped with designers' initials. They chatted over the shopping bags that sat between them as they ate quiche and mushroom salad off of styrofoam plates.

A woman with an apron was walking towards me. She seemed ready to take my order. I would have to tell her I was waiting for someone.

"Excuse me," she said. "Are you Maureen Lynch? I'm Sheila, Sheila Bornstein."

"Hi," I said. "I was expecting you to come from the other direction."

"Sorry," Shelia laughed. "I guess I forgot to tell you I work here. I try to forget it myself. I'm on my break now. Let me go get us some hot cider."

Sheila returned with the cider. She carried the tray in front of her as she made her way between the tables. She had on a long denim skirt, dark tights, and clogs. Her dark hair curled about her head as it fell in different lengths to her shoulders.

"I forgot to ask you," she said. "Do you want anything else? I just made some quiches this morning."

"No, thanks. This is fine," I said as I took a drink of the cider.

"I didn't realize I hadn't told you I work here; I'm the cook," Sheila said. "We just moved here. I finished my Masters at Boston University last spring. I'm from Boston originally." She went on to tell me that her boyfriend had gotten a fellowship at the University of Washington. She came along thinking she would have no problem finding a job. Though I sympathized with Sheila, it made me feel better about our own lack of success.

We began to talk about Mary Fran. When Sheila asked for a general idea of her interests I told her that she enjoyed crafts, bowling, bicycling, and travel. "The two places she most wants to go are Hawaii and Africa," I said. "She loves looking at *National Geographic* magazines."

"She sounds like a very interesting person," Sheila said.

"Oh, she is!" I agreed. "But I don't suppose most people see her that way when they first meet her. She's very quiet with strangers." I told her that Mary Fran would often just stare at the floor. She'd seem oblivious. Then after the people would leave she'd ask all sorts of questions and comment about what they had said.

"She's very astute about people," I continued. "She has

embarrassing our mother down to an art form. If they had an argument or disagreed about something, she'd wait until they were in public–preferably a large shopping mall–and then suddenly become very exaggerated, do some face grimaces or hop-skip dances."

Sheila laughed and asked, "Does she ever try that with you?"

"Once she did," I said. "But now she's found a more effective approach for me. She knows that doesn't embarrass me. The one time she tried it I bunny-hopped all the way through the mall and out to the car. She was furious that I would do anything so stupid. But I think she was mainly mad that I had upstaged her. She got back at me," I added.

"What did she do?" Sheila asked.

"It was awful," I answered. "The whole ride home she mumbled 'Stupid sister . . . dumb Mo . . . Look like fool!' And I hate that kind of droning, it's my pet peeve. She realized she was on to something when she saw all my little nervous tics come out. So now when she wants to get at me she whines. I hate whining!"

We talked a while longer. Then we agreed to meet the next week at our house. Sheila had said she'd charge eight dollars an hour. She had suggested two hourly sessions a week. That would be an extra sixteen dollars a week expenses. Sixteen times four . . . sixty-four dollars a month. We had taken six thousand dollars with us for our year's expenses. Our monthly expenses for the two of us were around $500. Sheila's lessons would be a chunky addition. But it would be worth it if she could teach Fran how to read.

On the way home I decided to stop and see Philip. It seemed like trying Sheila would be a good idea. If it didn't work out there was no commitment to continue. But I wanted to talk it over with Philip. The burst of determination that had propelled me to Seattle was beginning to wear thin. And all the decisions that had to be made were starting to bog me down.

Philip was at the kitchen table with books and notepads

spread out in front of him. He was studying for an accounting class he was taking at the community college. Seeing the clients he worked with return again and again to be hospitalized made him feel discouraged. Philip had begun to feel not only useless in his job, but he also felt abused because of his low salary. The salary had never bothered him before but he had recently decided that he didn't want to spend the rest of his life on an income that would limit him and Betty to studio apartments and dollar movies. As if he were trying to fight an earlier idealism that had betrayed him, he had suddenly started stressing "the practical" and questioning "the financial implications." He sat at the table with the accounting books spread out in front of him.

"What's up, Mo?" he asked as he pushed his glasses up and brushed his hair off his forehead. Philip was ten years older than I, but his auburn hair and freckles made him look more my age. He looked sort of like a grown-up Howdy Doody.

I told him about my meeting with Sheila. "What do you think?" I asked.

"That's something you should get into," he said. "Eight dollars an hour, huh?"

"That's not what I meant," I said. "I mean what do you think about trying a tutor?"

He agreed with me that we should try Sheila for a month. I told him that I was worried about finding Mary Fran a job, I was afraid that I had misled her to think that it was possible.

"Why don't you get her to try a volunteer job?" he suggested. "A lot of people do that to get experience and collect references."

"I already asked Fran about that," I said. "She said she didn't want to volunteer, that she wanted a paying job."

"Who doesn't?" scoffed Philip. "Just explain that it's harder than you thought it would be. She's had a chance to see for herself—with Christina . . . me, taking these damn classes . . . everything. Put a time limit on it so it won't seem so bad, like 'try this for two months.' In fact, why don't you go over to that rest home across the street. She would already know the bus routes."

"I'd love to get it settled," I said. "Even if it were just for a few months."

"Where is she now?" he asked. "It's so strange not to think of her as always being with one of us."

"She's at the Kiwanis Center," I answered. "She joined a two-week workshop, a kind of combination Goal Clarification and Assertiveness Training."

"I can't imagine Fran clarifying her goals in front of strangers," Philip laughed.

"I guess she isn't very verbal," I agreed. "The woman who's leading it called me after the second day."

"Oh no!" he said.

"Yeah, our sister almost got kicked out of an assertiveness training workshop for not being assertive enough."

"What did you say to her?" Philip asked.

"I dug up all the expressions I could remember from my psychology classes," I admitted. "I told her I could appreciate her concern, but that I felt the supportive environment of the workshop would be conducive to Mary Fran's growth. That she had led a very sheltered life, and to prevent an ambiotic relationship from developing between us, I wanted to allow her exposure to as many varied, healthy relationships as possible."

"You mean 'symbiotic' relationship'," he corrected. "She must have thought you were crazy."

"It doesn't matter," I said. "Professionals always think family members are crazy. Anyway, she let her stay."

As I was leaving Philip said, "Oh, yeah, Betty wanted me to ask you guys if you'd come over for Thanksgiving. We're just going to have some friends from the hospital and you three."

"Oh, good!" I said. "Do you want us to bring anything?"

"No," he said. "Just your own food."

"I know, 'Turkeys don't grow on trees.' "

As I walked to the bus stop we shouted down the sidewalk,

exchanging corny jokes, the kind Betty had disgruntledly come to associate with her in-laws. They were also the kind that I recalled from earlier years, the kind that had distracted us from jokes where Mary Fran was the punch line. Our jokes were usually started by Dad. Sometimes the pace was fast and mocking. Other times they were just painfully silly. But they were never any more silly or painful than the constant ups and downs that were our life with Mary Fran.

By the next week Shelia had started with Mary Fran. She was going to meet with her on Tuesday and Friday mornings. Also, a speech therapist was volunteering at the Kiwanis Center one night a week. She had taken Mary Fran on as one of her students. It was a busy week. Encouraged by the addition of Sheila and the speech therapist, we took Philip's advice and went to the rest home near his apartment.

A woman at the front desk of the rest home told us to talk to the occupational therapist, Chris Vidmar. Chris was also the coordinator of volunteers. She suggested that Mary Fran start out with a part-time schedule from ten until three. She smiled at Mary Fran and told her that she was glad to have her help.

"Especially during the holidays," she added. "We always get so busy because of extra visitors and additional craft projects."

Mary Fran said, "Oh," and then quickly returned her gaze to her shoes.

I felt like shaking her. She was so demanding of me. When I had suggested a party to celebrate her job she had refused, thinking I was being patronizing. And so many times after that she had demanded that I be honest with her. Now here we were together and she had backed out on me. Slipping into her retardate schtick she had left me alone to handle Chris. "Why don't you tell her you're capable," I had felt like saying, "It's people like her you have to convince, not me."

Even though it was a volunteer job it was a relief to have come up with something. We stopped on the way home to get lunch bags and cold cuts at Safeway. For the first time

I resisted the urge to give a lecture on nutrition. And I let Fran get everything she wanted, instead of bombarding her with wheat berries and yogurt. As we wheeled the cart down the aisle we both felt like we were celebrating. "Baggies," "Oliveloaf," "Twinkies." They sounded like shouts of congratulations. Mary Fran was joining the ranks of the workaday world!

At the end of the week Mary Fran got a call from Evelyn. She wondered if Mary Fran would be interested in trying out a new Chinese restaurant. When the answer was a quick yes, Evelyn said, "Great, I'll see you tonight."

That evening when they returned home Mary Fran was delighted with the evening out. She went upstairs to use the bathroom.

Evelyn turned to me and said, "She couldn't go to the bathroom alone in the restaurant."

"Oh, you mean because she didn't know which one was the women's?" I asked. "I guess we're just used to telling her which side it is or going with her."

"I don't know why it surprised me," Evelyn said as if she were angry with herself. "You told me she doesn't know how to read. But she just looks so normal. She is shy. But once she begins to trust you it's obvious she's quite capable."

"Did something happen?" I asked.

"She went by herself to the bathroom," she said. "And then I decided to go, too. And there she was, standing in front of the door marked 'storage.' I guess she had tried the door and when it was locked she thought there was someone inside. So she was just waiting."

"When we got back to the table," Evelyn continued, "I had to read the menu to her. It hit me, all of a sudden, just how vulnerable she is."

Before she could say anything else Mary Fran came down the stairs. From that first month on, Evelyn and Mary Fran usually got together once a week. Sometimes they took drives out to hiking paths like they did that first day. Or they'd try out new restaurants. But usually their times together were much less structured—Evelyn would be baking and she'd call Mary Fran to join her. Or they'd get together to do some errands at a nearby shopping mall. Or Evelyn would be baby-sitting for her grandson and she'd stop by to show him off.

Having a friend was new to Mary Fran. When she was living at home she went to a school that involved a three-hour bus ride everyday. Once she got home, her friends were scattered throughout the area. The thing was that Evelyn was sharing her life with Mary Fran. Evelyn was the first person who had reached out to Mary Fran who wasn't a family member or a teacher. Evelyn was being a friend.

CHAPTER 12

Christina and I got a letter from Terry, a friend of ours from college. He told us that he'd be arriving in Seattle in early December. Carleton College had revamped its calendar in an attempt to save fuel during the severe Minnesota winters. The result was a six-week winter break. Terry decided to use that time to take us up on our invitation to visit. He had his civil service scores transferred to the Seattle postal department. And he soon received a letter confirming that he had been accepted for a temporary position for the holidays.

We were both looking forward to having him with us. I realized that one of the reasons I was so relieved to have a fuller schedule for Mary Fran was because I wanted to look good in front of my friends. Our friends from college who were from the Northwest were returning to spend the holidays with their families. Letters had been exchanged and we had offered our house as the rendezvous spot.

Terry would be staying with us for a month. Mark, Terry's roommate, would be staying with his family in Portland, but he'd be visiting frequently. Debbie and Carol were taking winter term off to hunt bugs in Costa Rica for their senior biology projects. Carol would be staying with her family in the Seattle area. And after their trip they were going to be visiting us.

As I thought of everyone from college to whom I had written during the fall, I remembered their confusion about what I was doing. The reactions had been variations of "Aren't there programs for people like her?" and "What could you possibly do to help her, you aren't even a certified teacher?"

The question that usually made me most frustrated was why did we have to move to Seattle from our home in Michigan. The answer that Seattle had more to offer Mary Fran never seemed to satisfy them. This seemed so ironic to me, since my friends and I had all spent most of eleventh grade pouring over college catalogues. Location seldom deterred us in our search for a college.

I tried to explain that Mary Fran was very outgoing and confident when with her family. But in other situations she is often self-conscious and quiet. It's as if the new situation reminds her of the bulky terms she must carry around with her—mentally retarded. Or maybe she's just shy. Sometimes I watch myself in a new situation and marvel at what a backward clod I am. It seems ridiculous that she isn't even allowed to be, plain and simple with no further significance, a backward clod. Everything she does or doesn't do is sifted, sniffed, and analyzed, and in the end it's always traced back to her I.Q.

I tried to keep myself in tow when talking with my college friends. I often returned to the dorm with stories about special education programs I had visited with a class or in which I was tutoring. They would listen obligingly. I imagined them noting with an outsider's coolness, "Maureen has a keen interest in the handicapped." I tried, usually unsuccessfully, to swallow the words that came racing up my throat. I didn't want to be marked as too zealous, a dorm party bore.

Terry and I had been neighbors in the dorm our freshman

year. Now, his junior year, he had just declared his major as English and was looking forward to a break from departmental requirements and reading lists. Christina and I planned the first day—a tour of Ballard, a ferry ride, and a trip to the outdoor market downtown to get the ingredients for the communally-cooked dinner.

But when he and Mark arrived that Sunday afternoon they ignored our suggestion that they get back in the car so we could begin our tour. Both they and the car, a little orange Subaru, looked well traveled. Terry and Mark were bleary-eyed and shaggy. Christina and I had run out to greet them, looking forward to being brought up to date on fellow friends and the college life that seemed so far away.

They bent to stretch their stiff backs as they yawned the promise that they'd limit their nap to a few hours. Wrestling with the contents of the back seat they managed to pull out two sleeping bags. They mumbled an explanation about the bent fender that included the words "deer," "Montana," and "snow." Christina and I followed them dejectedly as they made their way up our steps and into the house. They only got as far as the living room where they rolled out the bags and immediately fell asleep.

Mary Fran came up behind me and, curious about the person who was going to be living with us for a month, asked, "Which one Terry?"

Looking at the two bodies that lay face down with arms spread out I pointed to the one on the left. "That one," I answered. "The blonde one."

"Oh," she said, "other one Mark?"

"Yes," I responded. "How do you like them so far?"

"Hard to say," Mary Fran answered, trying to be polite. But I'm sure she was wondering why Christina and I had been so excited about their visit.

That evening things began to look more promising as the five of us sat in the kitchen together. Christina and I had had to put our tour plans aside and settle for a trip to the local Safeway. Terry stood at the stove sautéeing onions for the shrimp creole. Christina, Mary Fran, Mark, and I watched Terry cook as we drank our wine and sat at the kitchen table pretending to be making the salad.

"Has Burt decided whether he's going to Carleton?" Mark asked, referring to Christina's brother who was a senior in high school.

"I don't know," Christina answered. "He's spending most of his time at the bowling alley. But if you could get him to be serious I think he'd admit he wants to go there."

"If you could get Doug to go, too," I said naming the fourth and youngest Karlson, "You'd have a whole family of Carleton graduates."

"What a disgusting thought," Terry said as he poured the stewed tomatoes into the skillet.

"You have big family?" Mary Fran asked looking at Terry.

Terry looked up as if wondering where the voice was coming from. No one said anything. Then Terry looked down again and busily began to stir the tomatoes and onions. "Yeah, it's pretty big," he said. "There are six kids."

"Boys or girls?" she asked. She seemed to be forgetting to be self-conscious.

"All boys except for one girl," he answered.

"What she think?" Mary Fran asked. "She like it, she like being only girl?"

I smiled at her question and looked at Terry wondering what he was going to say. But he didn't answer. He was looking at me and waiting. I recognized his expression. It was apologetic but at the same time expectant. He was waiting for me to interpret.

"Yeah, I'd like to know, too," I said. "What does she think about being the only girl?"

"Say again, Mo," Mary insisted, sounding as if she were mad at me. "He no understand." She didn't mind depending on me to be the interpreter as long as I didn't try to cover up my job.

"He understands," I said.

"Don't think so," she said defiantly.

"Well, ask him yourself," I said.

"You ask," she said.

"I already did!" I said. Then I suddenly became aware of the nervous fidgeting going on between Terry, Christina, and Mark. "You understand, don't you Terry?" I asked.

"Not all the time," he admitted. "The past five minutes I didn't understand either of you." He interrupted our laughter to add, "I didn't come here to be your houseboy. Somebody better start cooking the rice."

The next day I waited at the bus stop to see Mary Fran off to work. Then Mark drove Terry and me to the downtown post office where Terry would get his job assignment. We waited in the outer office while Terry went inside. When he came out he had a confused look.

"I'm unemployed," he said.

"But I thought you had been accepted as a temporary carrier," I asked.

"I thought so, too," he agreed.

Then he explained to Mark and me what he had just been told. It seemed they had overshot their budget, or something like that. They had promised more people jobs than they could now employ.

Mark decided to drop us off near the large department stores so Terry could apply for a job there. Then Mark would leave for Portland. He stopped at a red traffic light on the way to Frederick and Nelson's, the store that we were going to try first. And I wondered if the God of the Happily Employed had put a curse on me. I sure didn't seem to be a good influence on the people around me.

The three large stores that we went to—Frederick and Nelson's, Nordstrom's, and Bon Marche—all said they had already arranged for extra holiday help. On our way down to the Outdoor Market to get something for lunch we walked by Woolworth's. Terry was getting glassy-eyed from filling out applications and then being told, "Don't call us, we'll call you." He pointed to the door of Woolworth's that was decorated with red foil and plastic poinsettias. "One last try before lunch," he said apologetically.

We made our way through the crowded aisles and past a display of velvet paintings of nude women, and the Last Supper. Terry spoke with a clerk at a cash register who pointed to the back of the store. In the back he spoke with a man in a suit who gave him two pieces of paper and sent him to the lunch counter to fill them out.

"They have one more position left. They need someone to run the cash register downstairs in the toy department," he told me. "This is the 'test.' Look at it, you won't believe how easy it is. It's just basic math—addition, subtraction, multiplication."

"Oh, good," I said. "I'll just loiter around."

"It'll only be about five minutes," he said as he turned back to his test. He sat at the shiny stool at the front of the counter and quickly began to jot things down on his paper.

I walked down the aisle and looked at the wrapping paper and Christmas decorations. A clerk was busy taking down a display of pilgrims and turkey centerpieces. I wondered what kind of tree we'd get this year. We'd need a stand for it, I thought, as I looked at all the different kinds in front of me. I tried to figure out what kind was best.

"Honey, you best be finishin' quick, the man's gonna be back." I turned to see who had said that. A young woman at the lunch counter was talking to a fellow who leaned over a sheet of paper. He put his pencil down and leaned his head in his hands. They sat at the end of the counter squeezed closely together. The young woman looked like she was about my age. She had long, straight blonde hair and a very pregnant stomach. She continued talking to him, telling him how important it was that he get the job.

Then Terry came up behind me. "I have to go downstairs and give him the test back," he said. I moved on to look at other sections of the store. Terry was back in about ten minutes. He had a pamphlet, "An Employee's Guide to Woolworth's," and a tag that had his name on it.

"When do you start," I asked.

"Tomorrow," he said. "What a relief! He was really surprised that I got all the math problems right. He looked at me like I was some kind of freak."

I had known Terry would get the job. But I still felt mad at him for beating out the young guy at the end of the lunch counter. I thought of Mary Fran and realized that she would never get a job if she always had to compete with people like Christina and Terry . . . and me. I wanted to be little again and to be wearing one of the identical outfits that Aunt Irene always bought for Mary Fran and me. People would watch us as we played together, and they'd say, "How cute! They look so much alike, they must be twins."

We got in the habit of gathering in the kitchen every night and talking about what had happened during the day. One night there was an abrupt change of plans. Christina had declared the kitchen off-limits. Mary Fran didn't really mind. She left for the Kiwanis Center laughing at Christina and wondering what she was up to. But Terry and I sat in the living room and pouted.

"Oh, come on, Christina," I called into the kitchen. "If we can't come in at least tell us what you're doing."

"Definitely not," she said. "That's the whole point, I don't want you to know what I'm doing."

"All right, no more Mr. Nice Guy," Terry shouted at Christina. "We've indulged your silly whim. Now just exactly what is it you're doing?" Then he said aside to me, "I think what she needs is firmness."

We could still hear her bustling around in the kitchen opening and closing doors and containers. But now she began to laugh.

"Oh-oh, she's becoming hysterical," I said.

"Probably from lack of human contact," Terry added.

When Mary Fran returned that evening she hung up her coat in the closet. Seeing that the door to the kitchen was still closed she asked incredulously, "She still in there?"

"Yes," I answered. "I don't know what she's up to."

"You'll find out tomorrow," Christina called teasingly from the kitchen.

Christina was still in the kitchen when the three of us went to bed. That night I had a dream about a young woman with long blonde hair and a flowing white gown. She had a crown of lit candles on her head. And she stood next to my bed with some kind of tray and smiled gently down at me.

"I'm Saint Lucia," she told me.

"I know," I said calmly. I thought if I just agreed with her she would go away. I wasn't used to having religious dreams.

"I know it's you," I said and turned to the wall hoping she'd decide to leave.

"Maureen!" she called. Oh, my God, she knew my name!

"Maureen, you have to help me," she said.

I turned over to face her wondering what kind of straits Heaven was in that a Saint would have to go to Ballard for help. But when I rolled over what I saw was Christina standing in front of me with a sheet wrapped around her. She was putting the tray down on the floor.

"Maureen, you have to help me," she repeated as she peeled a piece of wax off her forehead. "The candles are dripping and I'm afraid my hair's going to catch on fire."

"Christina, what are you doing?" I asked as I slowly crawled out from under the covers.

Her face brightened and she ignored the dripping wax to answer my question. "I'm Saint Lucia," she said. "It's an old Swedish custom. The oldest girl in the family makes rolls the night before. Then—"

"Christina," I interrupted, "What time is it?"

"Five o'clock," she answered happily. "Come on, let's go wake up Mary Fran and Terry before the cocoa gets cold."

Then she bent to pick up the tray that had four mugs of cocoa and a plate of elaborately formed rolls with raisins and cinnamon—Saint Lucia Day buns. "I made them last night," she said smugly.

I reached for my glasses and was ready to go wake Mary

Fran and Terry. I decided that if I had to be awake, they might as well be up too.

But Christina said, "Wait, first I have to teach you the song."

It was pitch dark out. I was shivering as I stood there in my Special Olympic T-shirt. She stood facing me with the sheet wrapped around her, her hair and forehead being dripped on by the melting candles. We stood together in the middle of my bedroom trying to stay in the same key as Christina taught me the song.

"What are you two doing?" Terry asked as he stood in my doorway. Mary Fran stood behind him, looking as confused as he did.

"She's Saint Lucia," I said.

Then we started a verse of the song we had been practicing. Terry turned around as if he were going back to bed. When we finished the song Christina said, "Okay, now you each get a cup of cocoa and a Saint Lucia Day bun."

By six o'clock we had heard all about the Saint Lucia Day tradition, had learned the second and third verses of the song, and had eaten all the rolls. Christina left to change into the uniform she wore at the Norse Home. Because she walked to work, she would have to be leaving soon. Terry decided to go back to bed for an hour. I expected Mary Fran to, also. But she looked out the window at the pink sky and said, "Think me go for walk."

Three months earlier she wouldn't even stay in the living room alone. Whenever I went upstairs to the bathroom she followed and stood in the hallway. Now she was busing alone, but always with the security of a planned destination. I was delighted that she felt confident enough to go outside alone and just walk around the neighborhood.

"She went for a walk!" I told Christina as she pulled on her blue polyester uniform.

"That's nice," she said. "It was probably inspired by the Saint Lucia Day buns."

"She went for a walk!" I told Terry. He lay deep inside his

sleeping bag hoping the rest of the morning would be saint-free. "It sounds like a good idea. Why don't you go, too?"

I walked downstairs and sat on the window seat. Then I decided to sit on the sofa. She might have seen me and thought I didn't trust her. I changed places three times. Then I ended up back in bed pretending to be asleep.

CHAPTER 13

It seems like the main thing we did in December was cook. Outside the rain continued to pour down from the always-dark sky. Strong winds that rushed off the Sound would carry the rain around the house where it pounded at the shaking windows, and piled up on front porches. The four of us often would have to fight it out for who would get to use the stove.

One of the things Mary Fran was working on with Sheila was learning how to use picture recipes. They made applesauce, pancakes, and anything else they could get pictures together for. Terry was trying to duplicate his grandmother's holiday cooking and spent a lot of time making spritz cookies. Christina made us some of the Greek food she had loved ever since studying in Greece her junior year. And I was convinced that we could save money if we made our own bread. I branched out from whole wheat to cheese-chive, raisin-pumpernickel, and sour dough. It kept me busy, but it never saved any money. The butter would always be brought out and a whole loaf would be eaten while it was still

warm. The bad weather aside, we decided we should celebrate being in the Northwest. And so we began to experiment
with recipes calling for fish, like salmon, squid, and oysters.
Cooking was always a good excuse for inviting people over,
and sitting around together.

One evening Mary Fran looked around her. The Christmas
tree was up in the living room. Terry was baking. And Christina sat in the kitchen with him shellacking one of the leftover
Saint Lucia Day buns as a decoration for the tree.

"When we go home?" Fran asked.

"For Christmas?" I asked. "I'm not going home, I'm staying
here."

"Not me," she said. "Me go home."

"How are you going to get there?" I asked.

"Fly, only way can think of," she answered. "Take too long
any other way."

"We'll have to call Mom and see what she says," I warned.
"But she'll probably meet you at the Chicago airport. You
don't mind flying from Seattle to Chicago alone?"

"No way can help it," she said. But I thought I saw a faint
smile. I wondered if she was picturing coming off the plane
alone in Chicago and being greeted by Mom the way she had
always seen Philip, Patricia, and me do when we returned
from school or traveling.

"Fran's going home for Christmas," I said to Terry and
Christina as we walked into the kitchen.

"We'll have to have an extra special going-away dinner,"
Christina said. And we all reached for the cookbooks and
spread them out on the table as we began to plan the menu.

The next day we were able to get a reservation on a flight
for that weekend. With that settled we began to invite people
to the going-away dinner. We called Philip and Betty, Evelyn,
Sheila, Mark, and Carol.

"Is it safe to come in?" Philip asked as he stood at our front
door the night of the dinner. "Or is there an octopus lurking
in the kitchen?"

"Phil!" Betty admonished as she walked in the door in

front of him. "Don't pay any attention to him, y'all. I just said how much I enjoy tastin' the new dishes you gals are always tryin.' "

"That's not exactly the way you worded it, Betty," he corrected. "Remember? You were looking in the medicine cabinet for the Alka Seltzer because you said you were sure they'd be trying some strange, new recipe tonight."

Christina laughed and said, "We're having a very calm meal. No octopus, just lamb."

"Christina talked us into having a Greek motif," I said. "We're having moussaka, feta and olives, baklava, and ouzo."

"I can't believe it." Philip said. "We just had that last night!"

"Serously?" Christina asked. "You had moussaka?"

"Phil, what's gotten into you?" Betty exclaimed. Then she said aside to Christina, "He knows we didn't; he knows we had tuna-noodle casserole."

"Maureen," Terry called, "It's the phone."

Everyone went into the living room where they helped arrange the pillows on the floor, and put together the low, makeshift table we'd be eating on. I walked to the hallway where I picked up the phone.

"Hi," the voice said. "This is Ethel. Remember me from the Citizen's Advocacy class?"

"Sure," I answered. "How are you, Ethel?"

"Sick of shopping for Christmas presents," she answered. "But other than that I'm fine. I was wondering, are you and your sister going to be around for the Holidays?"

I had forgotten all about Ethel. I had been so relieved when Thanksgiving had come and gone without her calling me about visiting her brother at the institution.

"No, we're not," I answered. "My sister's leaving tomorrow to go home. And I'm going away with some friends next weekend. We're going to stay in a cottage on the Oregon shore."

"That sounds nice," she said. "When are you leaving?"

"Next Friday." I answered.

"Oh, good!" she said.

"Yeah, I'm looking forward to it," I said as I let Evelyn in the front door and pointed to the living room where everyone sat drinking wine and talking.

"Well, I'm glad you're not leaving until Friday," Ethel said. "Because I was hoping you'd be around this coming week. The social worker called and said we could visit my brother Tuesday." I didn't say anything so she added, "Will that be all right for you—Tuesday?"

We agreed that she'd pick me up at four. Pine Grove State School was far from town. I was glad she offered the ride, I didn't want to figure out the bus and transfers. I was so glad to have a ride that, as I said good-bye to her, I almost forgot I didn't want to go there in the first place.

The next morning Mary Fran and I were up early. It was still dark out as I carried one of her suitcases down the stairs. We got to the hotel downtown in time for the limousine to the airport. But when we got to the airport we saw a picket line from the airline Mary Fran was booked on. We found out that a strike had stopped all of their outgoing flights.

We rushed up to another airline's ticket counter. The woman behind the computer pushed some buttons, then said she could get Mary Fran on a flight the next morning.

"Well, that's not bad," I said as we walked past the picket line toward a bus to get back home. "At least you'll be getting out tomorrow."

"Have to call Mom," Mary Fran said.

"Yeah," I agreed. "She can get a room in a hotel and wait for you."

When we got home the phone rang. It was Betty wondering if Mary Fran seemed nervous at the airport. Everyone was concerned about her first flight alone. Mom and I had made jokes about synchronizing our watches. But we knew how nerve-racking it would be if she arrived and no one was there to meet her.

The next day, Sunday, we repeated our trip to the airport. There was a huge crowd at the ticket counter. Looking around I suddenly realized that there were huge crowds everywhere. People were sleeping on chairs, and families were camped out against walls. Then a man in an airline uniform came out from behind the counter. He held some papers and moved his arms trying to get attention.

"Look," he said, "I can't make any promises but the fog does seem to be lifting. Now, there are some flights that will be going out—flights 491 and 628 for Honolulu, *if,* and I have to stress '*if,*' the planes arrive from San Francisco.

His words were greeted by groans from the people who had pressed forward hoping to hear good news.

"Well," he added pointing to the picket line beyond the windows, "They aren't helping matters much. We're getting backed up. A lot of you folks were on their flights. And once the fog does lift we're going to have to accommodate all of their passengers by ourselves."

"Will there be any extra flights?" a woman next to me asked.

"I'd think so," he answered. "I can't make any promises, but I don't see how they could get everyone cleared out without adding flights. Where are you going?"

"Chicago," she answered.

"That might be a problem," he said. "O'Hare is having visibility problems on account of the snow. Some of the flights are having to land elsewhere."

"First things first," the airline worker said. "Now, what we're going to do is have everybody sign up on these priority sheets."

"Where?" a few people from the crowd asked as they pressed forward.

Three hours later we straggled down a hall in the airport carrying Mary Fran's suitcases as we tried to find a phone. I hadn't brought enough money for both of us to get home since I thought I'd be going back alone. We'd have to call Philip for a ride home.

Betty answered and said, "I already know. I saw it on the news, the crowd looks just terrible!"

"Yeah, it is," I said. "Can Philip pick us up? We don't have enough money for the bus service."

"I'll be there," she said. "Don't you worry. How is she?"

"Tired," I answered. "We're both very tired."

We called Mom that night. She hated being on call, it made her feel like she was missing out on the action. After I repeated everything I could remember the airline representative saying, she was finally satisifed.

"I'll stay one more day," she stated. "Then I'm going home; there's no reason for me to stay around here. Call me when she gets put on another flight."

Mary Fran and I were exhausted. We had gotten up at five the past two mornings only to spend the entire day pacing around the airport. When Betty dropped us off at home that evening we went straight to bed. The phone rang later that evening and I stumbled down the stairs to answer it.

"Mo, listen," Betty said. "I just heard on the eleven o'clock news that the fog is expected to lift. Y'all get up early and I'll drive you to the airport."

So the next day we repeated our act. Actually it was almost identical—we got up at five, the airline fellow said he couldn't make any promises, we all groaned in unison, the fog stayed where it was, and we returned home.

That night on the phone Mom said tersely, "I'm going home. There's no reason for me to hang around here. Call me at home if the flights start going out."

But Betty had other plans, she was determined. She picked us up at five on Tuesday morning. We scooted through the chilly morning blackness, as Betty insisted there was much better visibility. Then she outlined the battle plans—"We're going to be assertive!" she declared.

Mary Fran finally did get on a flight around noon. Mom received the news by angrily asking, "Why didn't you tell me the fog was going to clear? I would have stayed in Chicago! There's no way I can make it back there in time now."

I had hardly slept in four days and she wanted accurate weather predictions! We remembered that friends of the family lived near the airport and would be able to meet Mary Fran's plane while Mom once again left for Chicago.

The next day Mom called to say that it was a difficult flight all the way around—delayed in leaving; it was late to arrive; when it finally did land the first person off was a man on a stretcher who had died of a heart attack en route.

But I didn't know that as Betty dropped me off. I thanked her for her help the last couple of days. And I made a promise to myself to never make any more southern belle jokes about her. She was in a hurry to get the car back to Philip, who needed it for one of his classes. Christina and Terry were both at work so the house was empty. I walked into the kitchen to get something for lunch. I leaned over the sink washing the lettuce and looked at the calendar. The day, December 23, was marked "4:00–Ethel." I had forgotten all about it. In a couple of hours Ethel would be by to take me to Pine Grove.

Ethel turned into the driveway of Pine Grove. It had a sign out in front with script lettering that made it look more like an entrance to a condominium than a state institution. There were a series of large brick buildings with barred windows. We walked into the administration building. A guard who was sitting behind a desk near the front door told us how to get to the social worker's office.

The hallway was empty. A few people were in the office we passed. There was the quiet hum of typewriters, voices, and footsteps. As we turned a corner a young man came out of one of the offices. He offered to take us to Ethel's brother. He said the social worker Ethel had talked to on the phone had to go downtown to a meeting.

We followed him down a long, narrow, covered walkway that connected the administration building with one of the other buildings. At the door he stopped and unlocked the door, then opened it for us.

Inside was a huge room the size of a gym. It was full of beds lined up next to each other, row after row after row.

The white sheets were all tightly pulled across the beds. And the room, with its green cement walls, was completely empty. The social worker led us through the beds to a small office in the back. Two ward attendants were sitting in the room smoking. It was a small, glassed-in office with room for only a file cabinet and shelves for the many medications. He asked about Ethel's brother. After checking on a list, one of the attendants told the social worker, "Building E."

We continued through a series of locked rooms similar to the first one. Finally we came to "Building E." It was the first one with any people in it. Off of the huge room with beds was an area with a TV, a drain in the middle of the linoleum floor, and about fifty or sixty people. The social worker walked to the other side where an attendant stood leaning against the wall. Ethel and I stayed near the door.

Looking closer I realized they were all men who seemed to be in their twenties and thirties. Most of them sat near the TV, where many rocked in rhythm to the game show tune. They all had on gray cotton drawstring pants and grey slip-over shirts. Above the blare of the TV could be heard some screeches and sing-song repeated phrases. A short, chubby young man rocked by us, taking one step backward for every three forward. "See ya later," he chanted in rhythm "See ya later, see ya later, see ya later . . . " When he got near us he said his phrase while looking straight at our faces. Then he let out a huge laugh as if it were some fantastic joke.

The group at the TV watched us suspiciously. Then one of them suddenly looked at Ethel and screamed, "Mommy!" as he began to run toward her.

"Oh, my God, is this him?" Ethel asked.

She held back tears as she looked at him, then around the room. Looking down at the young man, who was smeared with feces and had wrapped himself around her, she asked, "What's your name . . . Come on, tell me. What's your name?"

A man in gray came toward us with a mop held in his

hands. He had been cleaning up one corner of the room, but stopped to watch Ethel.

"His name's Ronald," he said as he roughly grabbed the young man away from Ethel. "But he don't know that, he don't know his name."

At that the group around the TV let out a howl as if they were some strange Greek chorus. "Ronald!" "Gonna get the shit beat out of you!" "Ain't good for nothin' but shit!"

The attendant came out of the office with the social worker behind him. "Dave!" he called.

The man with the mop let go of Ronald and turned, "Yeah?" he asked.

"You've got visitors," the attendant told him pointing to us.

On the way home Ethel asked me to stop for a drink with her. So we stopped at a little bar in Ballard full of fishermen.

"He seems so normal," she said.

I didn't know what to say. I felt like defending the others by explaining institutionalized behavior to her. But I knew this was no time to play sociologist.

"That damn doctor!" she said meaning the pediatrician who had advised her mother.

"Yeah," I agreed. "They all used to say that, 'Put him away.'"

Then we both fell silent. We both seemed to suddenly feel uncomfortable. As if we had just gone through something very intimate, and then just realized how little we really knew each other.

When I got home there was a note from Terry and Christina—"Did Mary Fran get on a flight? We went to a film. If you want to join us meet us at the University at 7:00." I rummaged around in the kitchen trying to figure out what to have for dinner. I settled on a handful of peanut butter cups and some Washington State Rosé. I took my dinner and a lawn chair from the kitchen out to the front porch where I put my feet up on the railing and watched the rain splatter down. I thought how delighted Christina would be to catch me eating candy after all my tirades about white sugar, white flour, and junk food. Then I remembered Mom's frantic reaction earlier in the day to my excited news that I had finally been able to get Fran on a flight. And I kept picturing parts of the institution we had visited. God, people are disgusting, I thought as I stuffed another peanut butter cup in my mouth.

CHAPTER 14

Terry had to leave at the end of December to go back to school. One of the last weekends Mark drove up from Portland, and the four of us squeezed into his car for our drive to the Oregon shore. It was raining, just like Seattle. But it was a gentler rain, sometimes it turned into a light mist. The ocean rolled in under the heavy gray sky. We wore shorts as we hiked in the woods and walked along the shore. I wished Mary Fran were with us; she'd have loved it.

The wet, gray Northwest weather that had seemed depressing when I first moved there had begun to seem comfortingly familiar. Sort of protective, like living inside gray fluff. Our last night we lay in front of the fireplace. We could hear the waves breaking on the beach outside. I was reading one of the James Joyce novels Terry had brought with him. Christina and Mark and Terry were playing Botticelli. I was glad Mary Fran wasn't there. It was such a relief not having to worry about defending her, translating for her, being strong for her.

On Sunday we packed up. Mark and Terry got ready for

their trip back to Minnesota. "Only two more terms," Terry reminded Mark as he carried his things out to the car.

"And I only have six more months of 'domestic tranquility,' " I said.

"And I've probably got about 200,000 more bed pans to empty," groaned Christina.

When Christina and I returned to Ballard it seemed strange not to have Fran with us. She had decided to stay in Michigan for about three weeks so that she could celebrate her birthday, January 15, at home. Though it seemed strange to not have her there, I wasn't looking forward to her coming back because that would mean starting job hunting all over again.

Once we had gotten the job problem settled it had been a very temporary solution. On Mary Fran's last day at the rest home the director of volunteers, Chris Vidmar, had called us in to thank Fran for her help. She handed her a nice reference, but explained that after the holidays there wouldn't be anything for her to do. The young woman looked at Mary Fran with concern and said, "I wish I could do more. I really do. Well . . . good luck."

It had ended the way we had expected it to. But we were suddenly both very somber. We knew that once she got home from Michigan in January we'd have to start all over again. Not really all over again, I tried to remind myself. She was so much more confident than when we had come in the fall. And it wasn't just a matter of attitude. There were real changes, new skills. In fact, she had already mastered many of the things I had hoped she would learn before the year was up. Then why did we both feel so swamped?

That day we had come home and both immediately gone upstairs to our separate bedrooms. Once in my room I reached for my journal and started writing. I imagine Fran was bustling around in her room straightening things up. She always did that—tightened up her sheets, brushing out every wrinkle, and lined up objects to perfect symmetry. I had once told Christina that it seemed to be the only area

Fran had control of. People were constantly deciding for her, moving her around, or limiting her. But when it came to her bedroom and the bathroom shelves, she ruled supreme.

At home we could always tell when she had recently left a room. Everything would be lined up in files, bottles behind jars behind books behind vases. Everything standing at attention in straight rows as if they were waiting to go to battle. Sometimes she would disagree with our placement of an object and move it to another area . . . or another room. And we'd have to go running around trying to find her calling, "Fran, come on, I have to leave. Did you move my . . . " Of course, sometimes she'd be accused unfairly. And the book had already been returned to the library, or the glasses would be in their case at the bottom of a purse.

But I remember Christina laughing at me one night as I walked into my room to find everything neatly lined up on my window sill. Fran was at the Kiwanis Center, and I had groaned, "How does she have time to do everything else and still line things up?"

"Well, the way I see it," Christina said parroting my words back to me, "is that this is one of the few areas she actually has control over. . . . "

"Very funny," I said. "Enough of the theories, just help me find my glasses."

"They're not up here," she answered. "She put them in the living room on top of your pile of books. That's actually a much better place for them."

That afternoon I remembered our conversation and put my journal and pen down to go into Fran's room. She was standing near the window folding a blanket before putting it back at the foot of her bed. The window rattled as the rain continued to pound against it. It was so dark outside that Fran had her light on even though it was still afternoon. It seemed like we both were trying to make sense of things, trying to put some order into them, me with my journal and Fran with her straight lines and unwrinkled sheets. I didn't see why we couldn't do it together.

"Fran, let's make a list," I suggested.

"What kind of list," she asked, not wanting to get dragged into another one of my strange lessons.

"Just wait here," I said. "I'll go get some paper."

So that afternoon we had sat together and made a list of all the things we had both done that year that were new. I said ferry ride and she said making pancakes with Sheila . . . and the list went on: met Christina, cooked squid, ate figs, hiked with Evelyn, rode the bus alone . . . Our list became like a scrapbook, as we stopped to laugh and talk about specific incidents.

Then Fran remembered she had promised Pat she'd bring cookies for something that was going on at the Kiwanis Center that night. So we went into the kitchen to make a batch of peanut butter cookies. We were both in a great mood as we started getting things out for the cookies. I said, "I'll get the flour, and you get two-thirds of a cup of peanut butter." When I looked over at Fran I saw that she had a full cup of peanut butter. "No, Fran, I said *two-thirds* of a cup." "Oh, this not right," she said quickly as she began to put some of the peanut butter back. I poured the flour into the bowl and then looked over at her. This time she had less than a half of a cup of peanutbutter. "Two-thirds," I said sharply.

Then I heard myself. "Two-thirds," that was a fraction, a mathematical concept, a percentage of the whole. Of course she wouldn't know what it meant. But it's used so often in everyday life. You're just expected to know it. You have to know it. I had never noticed her having problems in the past when we cooked together. She's had to compensate for so many things that she must have focused in on any quick cues I unconsciously gave her, like pointing to a place on the measuring cup. Or if I said "only one-third," she'd hear the "only" and know that it must not be very much. But through the years she's not the only one who's been compensating. We've come to automatically edit activities so that we give her the parts we know she can do. Maybe I had just automatically always given her the measurements that didn't in-

– 118 –

volve fractions. It was all so involved. All we wanted to do was make some cookies. Who was it who kept planting these traps for us, making everything so complicated.

It's a good thing we have a vacation, I thought as I walked up the hill to our house. When you get to the point where making peanut butter cookies seems unsurmountable, you need time out. Nearing our house I shifted my bag of groceries as I reached for the house key in my pocket. When I looked up I saw that Sheila's car was in front of the house. She sat on our front porch where she was reading a magazine.

Then she looked up and said, "Shame on you, you're late!" Seeing that I was alone, she asked in surprise, "Where's Mary Fran?"

"You're early," I said, "like two weeks early."

"Oh, I forgot all about that," she said. "Michigan, right?"

"Want to come in anyway?" I asked. "Have you had breakfast?"

"Oh, please," Sheila said, "no breakfast. But I might as well come in, I don't have my next student until eleven."

Sheila sat at the kitchen table as I unpacked the groceries and put them away. Since she was there, I decided to ask her if she had any ideas on a job for Fran.

"I'd ease up on that if I were you," she advised. "I mean, look at me. I spent two years in graduate school thinking my Master's would make me marketable, and I still don't have a job."

"I know," I said. "I agree. But she's so determined, she keeps swaying me."

"What I don't understand," Sheila said, "is why you guys came all the way out here. I mean, I know she was having problems. But this was a pretty drastic move."

"It didn't happen overnight," I said. "When I was a junior in high school Mom decided she'd sell the house. She wanted to move to a bigger town where there would be more for Fran. And she was thinking of going back to nursing. But a lot of the programs she wrote to had lost their funding. Or else Fran wasn't ready for the other ones. It dragged out to four years—that's a long time to wait."

"But what did the doctors say?" Sheila asked. "You told me your parents took her to the diagnostic clinics. They must have come up with something."

"You can take your pick," I said. "Just about everyone can back up their theory, it depends on which evaulation you want to believe. My parents always clung to the one by Helmer Myklebust."

"Helmer Myklebust!" Sheila said. "You're kidding, *he* really evaluated Fran?"

"Yeah, when they took her to his clinic, he said she was brain-damaged and needed language therapy. And that she definitely shouldn't be considered mentally retarded or emotionally disturbed."

"So she started language therapy?" Sheila asked.

"Oh, sure!" I said. "Tell me where in the 1950's parents could find that. I mean, that was the problem. Dr. Myklebust had said exactly what my parents wanted to hear. But once they got home there was no place for them to go to follow his recommendations."

"Boy, it must have been hard on your Mom," Sheila said. "Oh, I have to go, look at what time it is! See you in a couple of weeks."

Sheila and I never had the time to talk. Except for our first meeting at Pioneer Square, Fran was always with us. That was fine with me, I didn't see what good dwelling on past evaluations would do. But it had never occurred to me that Sheila might think our coming to Seattle was on a whim. I thought she understood that everything else had been tried. I wondered if Evelyn knew, or did she think of us as a hysterical family who overreacted.

After the evaluation with Dr. Myklebust there were numerous EEG's because of her seizures. Then a few other doctors. And by 1960 she had started at Our Lady of Providence. Seven years later when she moved back home she was placed in the county-based program that was called TMR level, Trainable Mentally Retarded. A school psychologist had talked with Mom about eventual placement in an institution. It was considered realistic at that time, the late 1960's. The same psychologist is probably now doing evaluations on people in institutions as they are being taken out and placed in the community. And instead of "realism" he would be espousing normalization. Mom had come home from meeting with him in a furious mood. She spit out the name of the state institution he had offered giving her a tour of, stressing that she must be realistic. But Mom must have behaved herself because his evaluation reads that the "mother was an articulate woman who seemed to have reasonably realistic goals for her daughter."

When I was in high school and getting ready to go to college, we began to look at programs for Fran, too. In another year she would be automatically moved from the classroom to the sheltered workshop next door. The staff there was hard working. Many of them were parents who had started the school in the 1950's without any help from the school board. Mom belonged to the parent group. And I was in the youth group made up of high school kids. We organized Special Olympic meets, planned holiday parties, and photocopied reams of what we called our "public education campaign" material–fliers that we thought would eventually change, not necessarily the world, but at least Van Buren County.

So the sheltered workshop was a familiar place to us. It housed the Thursday night meetings for Mom when Fran and I would go along to have dances in the workshop while the parents talked in the classroom. And we'd meet there on Sunday afternoons when we had our softball games. Mom would go along to sit with the other parents under the trees as they collected everyone's dishes and bowls for the potluck dinner that would follow. But no matter how friendly and familiar a place Arlington Workshop was, we still hoped Fran's future would offer her more than that. They tried to do piece work when they were able to get contract work from the local industries. But most of their time was spent working on the braided rugs and cutting boards that were sold at the county fair. Maybe that would have been enough for Fran if we had kept quiet. Many of the people at Arlington thought so.

When I was a junior in high school we spent a weekend looking at a college I was interested in. A month later we visited an independent training program for Mary Fran. When I was a senior, I was accepted by the college. Mary Fran had already been informed that the people she had been interviewed by didn't feel she had the necessary skills. They thought she needed more of a middle step first. So we waited. And while we waited Fran began half days in the workshop. Mom wrote to other programs. The file that held the numerous brochures kept growing. Many of the programs reported severe financial cutbacks, some had closed down, others offered no more than what she already had.

Mary Fran's change started slowly, but after two years her patience had waned. After a bus ride, with much younger school children, that usually lasted an hour and a half, she would spend most of her day sanding the cutting boards. When our group of high school kids had graduated and left for college the youth group became less active. So she no longer even had an ocassional dance to go to.

At home with Mom she let out her frustration, the bitterness that was welling up inside her. Every suggestion she heard became a statement that she was inferior. Every question directed toward her was twisted into a trick, an attempt to undermine. Reading our mother's face, she realized that the question, "Is it because I'm retarded?" caused her to wince. It had originally been a simple, sincere one. But it had become difficult to know if she was just using it as a weapon. One thing was certain. She now used it frequently, and it took on the belligerent ring of a teenager's cry, "Get off my back!"

The year before we moved to Seattle, Mom decided something had to be done; there could be no more putting off, no more depending on the future. She thought she'd start with a full medical checkup. After that she contacted a center called REACH, Regional Educational Assessment Center for the Handicapped. I remember her writing me at college about it. They scheduled psychological, educational, and speech testing as well as the mandatory parent counseling sessions. Mom was very hopeful. And at first things did go well. Some of the REACH staff sat in on Fran's day program, and made suggestions to the staff there. Mom tried very hard to listen to the suggestions of the young social worker in her twenties who worked with her on parent effectiveness techniques. She agreed to try many of the things that she suggested.

The staff at REACH seemed to enjoy working with the mother and daughter who were both such diligent students. But they had overestimated their welcome at Fran's program. One of the teachers eventually refused to incorporate any of their ideas. He began to take his anger out on the easiest person—Mary Fran. "They say I'm supposed to 'encourage' you to talk in class," he'd call to Fran from the front of the room. "Miss Lynch, I'm talking to you! So I just thought, if it's not too much trouble, would you be kind enough to share a few of your thoughts with us." Fran would sit at the desk with her shoulders stooped over and her eyes staring at her feet. But it didn't help her escape the situation. Her classmates' laughter would continue, and so would the teacher's comments. Fran would throw up before going to school, she'd beg to stay home. But she still maintained her loyalty to her teacher, refusing to say anything to Mom except when her anger forced her to spew out a few remarks.

But part of REACH's program required Mom to also sit in on some classes. One day when Mom was walking past the portables that the school board had given to house the county special education program, she stopped when she heard what sounded like an argument. It was Fran's teacher. The next morning as Fran complained of a stomachache, Mom said, "Would you mind staying home from school this week to help me with some of the spring cleaning . . . taking down the storm windows and a few other things." Fran never went back.

That spring Mom tried to find a job in the community for Fran. She offered herself and Fran as volunteers, thinking she could eventually ease herself out. But South Haven is a small town, and there weren't many alternatives. Everyone just wondered why Fran wasn't in school. The months passed and Mom decided that this was no better. Philip suggested that he take Fran camping for a few weeks. Mom needed time away from Fran to make a decision. But she also wondered if it was her fault, if she was such an awful parent that she was the cause of all Fran's problems. She had to find out how Fran would act with someone else.

I couldn't have expected Sheila to know that all that had happened. But to go through the whole story with everyone was too much. I stood up from the kitchen table and walked into the hallway to call home. Mom answered, and I said, "May to speak to Ms. Lynch,?" When Fran got on the phone I said, "Hi, Fran how are you?"

"Fine," she answered.

"How's Cole?" I asked, referring to our dog that she had named King Cole.

"Fine," she answered.

"Are you having a good time?" I asked.

"Yes," she answered.

"Is the lake frozen over?" I asked.

"Yes," she answered.

"Anything you wanted to tell me?" I asked.

"No," she answered.

"Let me think if there's anything I wanted to tell you. . . . Oh, yeah, Sheila came over this morning." I could hear her laugh so I continued, "I was coming home from Safeway and there she was, the silly goose, just sitting on our front steps waiting for you. She doesn't know what to do now that you're not here. So she came inside and waited until it was time for her next student."

Then Mom got on the phone and I asked, "How are things going?"

"Fine," she answered.

"What's new?" I asked.

"Not much," she said.

"You know," I said, "You two sound an awful lot alike."

"Well, Maureen!" Mom said in exasperation. It was the tone that meant you know I can't talk now.

"Okay, Okay," I said. "Twenty questions, just say yes or no. Have you run into anybody from Arlington?"

"No," she said graciously as if I had just asked her if she wanted dessert.

"What's she doing during the day?" I asked. "Oops, sorry, let me reword that. Is she finding things to do?"

"Fine, I'll see you later," she said.

I had never heard her use that answer before. While I was trying to figure out what it meant in decoded form she said, "Fran just took Cole for a walk."

"What's he doing inside?" I asked.

"We have to keep him on a leash," she explained. "Some of the farmers are shooting at dogs that are running loose. Did I tell you Patricia called? She said her restaurant was really busy over the holidays."

"So how's Fran been?" I asked again.

"Fine," Mom answered. "A couple of times she's said she was going to teach me how to cook like you."

"She's just playing us against each other," I said. "You told me she said on Christmas that she didn't think she wanted to come back here."

"Yes, I suppose that's it," Mom agreed. "There really hasn't been much to do. We've had some bad storms so we just play cards or watch TV. Other than that, we just go outside to get wood for the fireplace or take Cole for a walk."

"I have to get going," I said. "I'm supposed to meet Laura when she gets home from school."

"She's the girl you're an advocate for?" Mom asked.

"She certainly is," I said. "I wish I had gotten someone

simple. Did I tell you that Laura's father has been in and out of hospitals himself. He works in a sheltered workshop. And the mother . . . she's got her story down so well that no one believes her. It seems everyone in the city has been suckered in by her."

"So who do you believe?" Mom asked.

"I don't know," I said. "I called Laura's guidance counselor because I wanted to visit her in school. And she said Laura's mother was a 'professional parent.' And by the way she said that I don't think she meant she's active in the PTA."

On the bus ride over to Laura's house I thought about my last visit two weeks ago. We had made bread sticks. Actually, the three of us had made bread sticks. Mrs. Barnes kept flitting in and out of the kitchen nervously—"Here, Maureen, use this." "No, Laura not that way!" "It certainly smells delicious, girls." At first I thought she was just so happy to have someone for Laura that she was bustling around trying to smooth out any rough spots. But now it seemed like she was terrified to let go of Laura. I don't know what she was afraid would be said if she weren't there. But she continued to hover over us. This time, I vowed, we would go outside for a walk, a bus ride, shopping . . . anything but stay in that house.

CHAPTER 15

When Mary Fran got back from Michigan we *had* to find a job. We revisited the social service agencies feeling like worn soldiers visiting the sites of old battles. Again—nothing.

This time, however, we were influenced by what we had seen the past fall. Not only with Mary Fran's attempts to find a job, but also watching Philip, Christina, Terry, and Sheila. So when a social worker from the Office of Vocational Rehabilitation suggested the Northwest Center, a sheltered workshop, we began to consider it. Or at least I began to consider it.

We left the agency and looked around the Capitol Hill neighborhood trying to remember where the bus stop was.

What do you think of the Northwest Center?" I asked. "It sounds pretty good to me."

"Want a real job," Mary Fran said as she led the way to the bus stop and sat down at the bench.

"Well, they have all kinds of jobs there," I said. "You heard what he said. They get lots of contract work from companies. So you can choose from–"

"But it's a shelter workshop," she said, impatiently interrupting me.

"I know," I said. "But all sheltered workshops aren't the same. Let's at least go look at it."

We sat on the bus stop bench in a deadlock. Once we got home the debate continued.

"Look," I said, "You worked at the rest home for two months and got a nice reference. That was a very good experience. But now the holidays are over and they don't need you anymore. And jobs are hard to find."

"But me capable," she insisted trying to start a fight.

"Everybody's capable," I said. "That's the problem. You saw what a hard time Christina had and she's capable."

"Everybody not capable," she answered as she began to list students from her school at home. "Billy Selmer not capable, Josephine Ranton not capable. . . . "

"Okay, okay, I know what you mean," I interrupted. "But you're acting like it's up to me to decide who gets a job. It's not my fault, I've done everything I can think of."

"Maybe have trouble because not have B.A.," she said about me, as she paced the living room. Then she looked me over as if she were considering firing me. "Have high school diploma, but not finish college. Who knows why you stop. Maybe too hard, maybe you not capable."

"Fran!" I said. "You know why I stopped. I wanted to live with you for a year. Anyway, the people we've been going to all have their B.A.'s, and they can't help either."

"If me go there," she said, "what happen to Sheila? Her still come to tutor?"

"I don't know," I answered. "I don't see how she could. If you started working at the Northwest Center you'd be there all day. You'd just have time to get home for dinner before going down to the Kiwanis Center."

I knew Mary Fran looked forward to Sheila's visits. That was why I was having a hard time telling her that Sheila wasn't really doing much. I had sat in the living room one morning while Sheila and Mary Fran were in the kitchen

— 128 —

trying one of the picture recipes. I smiled as I listened to how easily Mary Fran talked with her. It was probably because her lessons completely lacked any demands that made Mary Fran so comfortable. But it also surprised her. I once heard her ask, *"N'tional Ge'graphic,* that all we do today–look at *N'tional Ge'graphic?"*

Sheila's interest seemed to be fading. She had been talking about a restaurant she and some friends wanted to start in Pioneer Square. But maybe it would be better, they had decided, if they started small with something like a frozen yogurt stand in the outdoor market. She and her friends, all transplanted easterners and all trained in some field of social services, had narrowed down their ideas and seemed determined to bring frozen yogurt to Seattle.

The idea of working in another sheltered workshop was not very appealing to Fran. But the suggestion that if she did, she would no longer be able to meet with Sheila was too much to take. She looked genuinely hurt, as if I had given up on her. She stalked out of the room and up the stairs mumbling that she was capable and that Sheila was a good teacher. I felt bad. But as soon as I heard her begin her mumbling, something I was sure she was doing because she knew how much I hated it, I began to feel much less guilty.

That week we went to the Northwest Center. The full name was the Northwest Center for the Retarded. The series of white buildings that housed it had once belonged to the Navy. The center was in an industrial area near other factories. That's all a sheltered workshop is, I tried to remind myself, it's a factory. The people who work in it are handicapped. But the assembling and packing are the same kind of work people all over the country do in factoies. I was fighting the same kind of bias Mary Fran was. Because of her bad experience at the sheltered workshop at home, we had all come to associate workshops with the worn-down, useless feeling that comes from spending your days doing busy work. It's true that some sheltered workshops don't have any real jobs and have to create busy work. But it's also true that many are busy and productive.

We walked by a building where a group of men were standing on a loading dock. One of the men started giving directions, and they began to lift crates into a nearby truck. Across the yard a group of toddlers poured out of a building. They were part of the center's Infant Stimulation class, a pre-school for handicapped children up to three years of age. Besides the Infant Stimulation program and the various workshops, the Northwest Center had classes for children too old for the pre-school and too young for the workshop.

The In-Take director, a young man named Stieve, showed us into his office. On the wall behind his desk were two posters. One said "Label jars, not people." The other one had a wheelchair and below it was written, "You gave us your dimes, now we want our rights." I looked over at Mary Fran as she sat stiffly in her chair next to me. The poor guy, I thought as I looked across the desk at Stieve. It's obvious that neither of us wanted to be there. And he probably didn't particularly want us either. I watched him look over the application we had filled out—Michigan, Michigan, Michigan, all her schools had been in Michigan. Then why, I expected him to ask, were we in Seattle?

"Well," he said as he looked up, "Would you like to have the grand tour?"

Neither one of us looked particularly enthusiastic as we politely answered, "Yes." He took us on a walk that went up and down some stairs and through narrow hallways. Some people worked on putting together ball-point pens, others were involved with machinery, and others packed and loaded boxes. It looked like a busy factory, not at all the kind of place we had come to associate with the term "sheltered workshop."

We walked into a room where the workers had pushed back their chairs and were taking a break.

"Donna, I've told you about smoking," Stieve said as he walked up to one of the workers who had lit a cigarette.

"Oh, Stievey," she answered. "Will you stop hassling me! I'm on my break. Jeez, the people around here!"

Then they both started laughing as if they were celebrating a well-rehearsed skit. The others joined in with laughter and shouts of "Stieve!" "Hey, Stieve, come over here!"

On the walk back to his office Stieve turned to Mary Fran and asked, "Well, what do you think?"

She said, "It's okay," as she continued to look down at the floor.

Dissatisfied with her answer he said, "It's a pretty good place. I really think it is. Don't you think so? It's pretty nice, isn't it?"

"Yes," she finally agreed quietly.

I watched him as he squeezed a "yes" and a smile out of Mary Fran. He didn't have an easy job. The people who worked in the workshop could at least get satisfaction out of their neatly piled boxes, their attempts to beat the clock in their piece work, and their checks that responded to the weeks when they were able to work faster. But Stieve didn't have neatly packed crates to measure his success. The people in the workshop had become his product. While they counted their pens, he counted their smiles.

The amount of control that staff had over Mary Fran had always seemed so unfair to us. It seemed almost sinister; they were able to refuse her the chance to fail. They could even refuse her the chance to try. But watching Stieve, I realized that was because her failure would be theirs, too. For as long as she was in their program she was their product.

The next week Mary Fran started working at the Northwest Center. The first week she excitedly talked about all the different jobs there were. On Friday she brought home a check for $21.75. At the bank she endorsed it with the stiff block letters that spelled her name. Then we went to a department store in Ballard where she bought some sweat shirts to wear for work so she wouldn't get her sweaters dirty. The contract work she did varied. She often came home with streaks of dirt on her clothes and her hands stained. At first

I asked her about work, and she would explain what they were doing. But her descriptions were always short, so I stopped asking. We both were glad to have arrived at some sort of solution. Neither one of us wanted to rock the boat.

After a week she learned the bus route to the Northwest Center. She was disappointed about not working with Sheila any longer. But she and Evelyn still got together every week. And she spent most of her evenings at the Kiwanis Center.

One night, when she was at the Kiwanis Center, Christina sat working on her quilt as I watched.

"Why don't you put that stuff away," I said. "And I'll teach you what I learned in my jazz dance class last night."

"No," she said. "I want to get this section done tonight. Why are you so antsy?"

"I'm not antsy," I said as I felt the plants to see if they needed watering. In the kitchen I filled a jar with water. As I bent over the plants to water them I said, "You know what I think it is?"

"What what is?" Christina asked.

"The reason I'm so antsy," I said. "I think it's the Empty Nest Syndrome. There's nothing for me to do now that Fran's at work all day."

"Poor, poor Maureen," Christina said sarcastically.

"Maybe I'll splurge and have a Tupperware party," I said.

"Or an affair with the mailman," Christina suggested.

"No, that's out," "He's from Carleton. He saw our mail from Terry and Mark and everybody and asked if we were alum. He's an English major, class of '72."

"*Uf da*," groaned Christina.

"What's that mean?" I asked.

"Oh, it just means . . . it's like the Swedish version of '*oy*.' "

The next day I was sitting in my room looking over the journal I had written in the fall. I had made a note of each agency and organization we visited and what the outcome had been. There was a note after the Bureau of Developmental Disabilities. I had forgotten about that. When we went to the BDD office, the social worker had said that he had no suggestion for Fran. But he said I'd be perfect for a pilot program that was supposed to start in January. They'd need tutors to go to people's homes. I had felt guilty that we were looking for Fran and I was the one offered a job. But I looked down at the phone number he had given me and decided to call and see if the program was started.

"I'm Barney . . . Barney Weber," he said as he came out from behind his desk that was stacked high with folders and notebooks. I had called him in the morning and he asked me to come over that afternoon. He said the program had started but that they still needed tutors. When I got to the Bureau of Developmental Disabilities office he explained that the Home Aide program offered families with handicapped children a visiting tutor, therapist, or just babysitter if that was what they needed. Then he looked over my résumé, and advised me to finish college.

"You've got a pretty good background here," he said as he looked over my résumé. "But it won't mean much if you don't get your degree."

I explained that I was just taking the year off, and that I would most likely continue for a graduate degree.

"One step at a time," he cautioned with a paternal smile. "First let's get the B.A."

I still don't understand what I was doing wrong that I couldn't make him understand. But every few weeks when I saw him at the office he would stress the necessity of finishing college. I imagine when I finally quit in June and we left Seattle, he breathed a sigh of relief, thinking he had finally gotten through to me.

The week after my first interview Barney called and asked me what I knew about cerebral palsy. "Not much," I admitted. He told me about a couple who had requested respite care for their eighteen-year-old son.

"It says here," he said as he talked to me over the phone, "that they'd like someone for about four hours one evening a week. It seems they belong to a church group. And let's see, about the boy . . . he has cerebral palsy, is severely mentally retarded, nonverbal, and nonambulatory. What do you think, would you like to go out and meet him?"

"I'm not sure," I said. "I don't know if I'd know what to do."

"Well, this is new to me, too," he said. "I used to work in child welfare before I got transferred here. But it wouldn't hurt for us to go meet the family."

I met him at the office and he drove us out to the Radtkes in a green car marked Washington State Social Services. He handed me the directions he had written down for getting to the Radtkes. He explained his second wrong turn by saying, "I've lived in Seattle all my life. The only time I left it was when I was stationed in the Pacific during the war. But the city sure is spreading out . . . now what does that say—northeast or northwest 176 street?" Eventually we made it, and Mrs. Radtke greeted us at the door. She was nervous, probably feeling she had to defend her son in front of the two strangers who would only see him as a living example of various terms.

"Well, I'm glad Tommy stayed home from school today," she said as she led us into the living room. "He's had a little bit of a cold, but now you have a chance to meet him."

A thin young man sat stooped over in a chair. One hand repeatedly banged an orange football against his leg. His two legs dangled, disappearing into high top black sneakers.

"Tom, look up. Oh, come on, this is no time to be coy!" Mrs. Radtke said as she leaned over him and brushed his bangs aside. "Alright if you want to be blasé," she said as she looked up at us and winked. "This is Mr. Weber and this nice young lady is Maureen. Isn't that a pretty name? She might be staying with you when Dad and I go to church."

Tom continued to bang the football against his leg.

"Oh, my goodness!" Mrs. Radtke said as she stood up suddenly and looked alarmed. "I forgot all about my T-shirts! Excuse me for a minute." As she started to rush down the basement steps she called, "I'm dyeing T-shirts for our Special Olympics team. Please sit down; I'll be right back."

When she came back she said, "They're really quite good—the kids at Tommy's school. He and I are the cheerleaders. But some of those kids would really surprise you!"

"Yeah, it's great," I agreed. "I've been a Special Olympic coach since high school."

"That's nice," she said.

"And my sister's run in a lot of meets," I added.

"Oh, well, then you understand," she said as she sat back in relief.

I listened to her as she gave me directions on how to change Tom's diapers, and I hated myself for not understanding. For wondering why she did it. What kept them from putting him in an institution? Suddenly the concerns my family had seemed like such luxuries. On the way home the only thing I could think of was the way she kept talking to him while he sat pounding his thin, dangling legs with the toy football.

Mrs. Radtke insisted that I call her every evening after I got home from the long bus ride from their house. She always asked about Mary Fran and Christina. If she knew that I didn't understand the life they had with their son it didn't make her angry. She had as much patience with me as she had with Tom.

The next family Barney Weber called me about was the Thorndikes, a young family with three boys, The youngest, a two-and-a-half-year-old, was in the Infant Stimulation program at the Northwest Center. David charmed me immediately. His parents were concerned that their two older sons were being ignored because of all the special attention David got. Even with that attention they still didn't have time for all the at-home work David's teachers recommended.

After meeting with his teachers I learned the exercises and games that David needed to do because of his cerebral palsy. My three visits each week freed the rest of the family for scout meetings, soccer meets, and the other things they had had to put aside. I wished there had been a Home-Aide program when Mary Fran was little.

One Friday afternoon I got home from working with

David. And I was exhausted. With his dimples and infectious laugh he often tricked me into prolonging games. It wasn't until I got on the bus to go home that I realized how much running, lifting, and cajoling I had done. Mary Fran arrived home from the workshop soon after me.

"Hoedown tonight, Mo," she called to me as she hung up her coat.

"Oh, that's right. I forgot," I answered.

"You not have to go," she said as she came into the kitchen.

"But I want to," I said. "I haven't been to the Kiwanis Center in a long time."

"Up to you," she said. "Some people like dances, some people not like dances."

"I like dances," I said. "But I've been running around all afternoon with that little boy, David. I wish you could meet him; he's so much fun."

"He crippled?" she asked.

"He can't walk alone," I answered. "At least not yet."

"That too bad," she said. "He probably capable though. Some people take more time. I bet his parents be tickle to death when he learn to walk."

That night Mary Fran and I went to the hoedown at the Kiwanis Center. I spent most of the night following her around. For once, I really was the little sister. I thought of all the years I was a coach to her athlete, a counselor to her camper, a teacher to her student. Gregarious, effervescent Mo! She must have hated me.

"Hey, Mary Fran!" called a young woman.

"Hi," Mary Fran answered quickly glancing over at me. "How you?"

"Fine, now that I'm here," she answered. "Doesn't this place look great?" she asked looking around at the decorations.

Watching them talk I recognized the young woman as Jenny. We had met her our first week at the Kiwanis Center. She worked at the day-care center, Happy Faces. But she was most proud of her new apartment. Mary Fran had told me all about it. She had moved out of a group home and into her own apartment a block from the Kiwanis Center.

"Who's she?" Jenny asked nodding at me.

"My sister," Mary Fran answered.

I remember answering that so many times when we were little–"Who's that?"

"My sister."

"How come she doesn't talk?"

"She talks! She just doesn't feel like saying anything now."

Then came the question that I always hated: "What grade is she in?"

Sometimes I would muster all my bravado to try to make it sound like I was sharing my wisdom with someone who was hopelessly out of it. Other times I would just mumble my way through the sentence, just wanting to get it over with: "She goes to the special school, they don't have grades."

At the end of the evening Jenny said, "You guys want to see my apartment?"

Jenny pointed to the building as we walked out of the Kiwanis Center. We were barely inside the apartment when a small, spotted puppy came racing across the room and skidded into Jenny's legs. She showed us her kitchen, which was decorated with Special Olympic ribbons. In the living room she showed us how her couch rolled out into a bed. Then she smugly showed us how much closet and counter space she had. It was one of the nicest apartments I had ever seen.

The next day Mom called. She had just gotten some information on a program in Nebraska. "Their residential program sounds great," she said. "And their job training program would be perfect for Mary Fran!" She added that it was nothing definite but that the realtor was showing the house that weekend. So maybe our house, that had been on the market for two years, was finally going to sell.

"Everything seems to be coming together," she added excitedly.

"It's about time," I said.

CHAPTER 16

Occassionally during the day the rain would stop. And the clouds sometimes cleared. This was Seattle's spring. At the end of March, Debbie and Carol returned from Costa Rica. Carol stayed at her family's house. Debbie stayed with us.

One afternoon they met me at the University of Washington campus after my film class. We walked between the buildings laughing as they told me about their experiences catching bugs for their senior project as biology majors. Eventually the conversation turned to Mary Fran.

"What I can't believe," Carol said, "is the difference in her from when I saw her last year."

"Yeah, that's right," Debbie agreed. "She came to Carleton with your Mom."

"And remember what she was like?" Carol asked.

"She just followed Mrs. Lynch everywhere," Debbie said. "And she didn't talk at all."

"Well, she didn't know anyone," I said quickly. "There wasn't much she could say."

"Cut it out, Lynch," Debbie said. "You don't have to defend her to us."

"That was close," Carol said with mock relief. "For a minute there I thought we were in for one of your 'The Mentally Retarded Are People, Too' lectures."

"Sorry, it's an automatic response. Anyway," I said baiting them, "I'm not very comfortable around intellectuals."

"Intellectuals?" grimaced Carol.

"That's ridiculous," Debbie said rising to the challenge. "You'll probably go to grad school before we do. We're just simple scientists. It's our job to risk our lives schlepping through remote areas as we study the intimate details of dangerous insects. In the meantime, Ms. Lynch will be groveling at some professor's feet as she churns out her dissertation."

"You're both disgusting," Carol said. "I have no delusions of grandeur. I'm going to work in a forest preserve. Or maybe a national park."

"Selling bumper stickers," Debbie added, "a noble calling."

"Let's get back to Mary Fran," Carol said. "What happens next year?"

"I don't know," I answered.

"But you were talking about that neat program in Nebraska," Debbie said. "Tell Carol about it."

"We found out that it's ending this spring," I said. "Their federal grant isn't being renewed. It had attracted all the superstars of the field. Now they're all going to different parts of the country, wherever they can get a job."

"I didn't know that," Debbie said quietly.

"We just found out last week," I said. "Mom was going to visit the place next month."

"So what happens now?" Carol asked.

"Mom is looking into group homes and job training programs that are near home," I said.

"So what does Mary Fran think about it?" Debbie asked.

"I haven't told her yet," I said. "I suppose I should. But I'm going to wait until Mom has some good news. I don't want her to waste the rest of the year worrying about having to go back to her old school."

"You mean she might have to?" Carol asked.

"No," I said, "Definitely not."

"But what else is there?" Debbie asked.

"I don't know," I admitted. "Maybe we'll have to stay here."

"But you have to finish college," Debbie said.

"I know," I said. "We'll figure something out."

The next week Debbie and Carol left for their last term at Carleton. They sent a note saying that their oral exam had gone well, but somewhere along the line they had lost one of the tarantulas. If you find him, Debbie added, please send him on to us.

Unfortunately, their note was not all we had to remind us of Debbie and Carol. We also had three squealing guinea pigs. Carol asked us to take care of the mother and two babies for a few weeks while her family was on vacation. We all looked forward to our babysitting assignment. So we were very surprised to find that we often wished we were taking care of the taratula instead. At least it would have been quiet.

When Carol had brought the guinea pigs over she explained their frantic racing around and nasty noises by saying, "You'll break them in, once they get used to you they won't squeal like that. They're just nervous." And she had picked the big one up to pet it, but it continued to squeal and tried to claw its way through her sweater heading for the front door. We could understand their nervousness. We told them that. But they continued to squeal. Everything made them nervous, the scraping of our lawn chairs against the kitchen floor as we sat down, the turning on and off of lights, everything! They never got used to us. Instead we often found ourselves sitting on the kitchen floor in the dark. Until we'd decide to assert our superiority as humans, then we'd stomp around the house, turning on lights and moving chairs.

Mary Fran and Christina looked forward to leaving for work in the morning. They'd smile as they headed for pigless territory. Sometimes I used the time alone to try to make peace with the guinea pigs. But it's not very encouraging to have your good will greeted by a squealing that increases in volume and pitch with your proximity. So I'd just stand there watching them as they frantically tried to burrow through the floor. Once I even tried to show my concern by giving them full run of the house. Instead of settling down on a nearby chair and expressing their gratitude, like a civilized pig, they became even more frantic and noisy. The house echoed with the scraping of little tiny pig claws as they searched for a place to hide. And for once their screeching was helpful as I used it to find them, digging them out from behind the stove and from under the toilet. I found myself looking forward to going to work, too. My only fear was that the Thorndikes and Radtkes would decide to get guinea pigs.

David's mother, Marge Thorndike, often talked to me about her concern for David's future. She knew that many people with cerebral palsy are often automatically treated as if they're also mentally retarded. Marge wanted to make sure that I knew that David wasn't mentally retarded.

She explained to me that he had been premature. She told me about the hospital staff's tests that led them to the dis- covery that David had cerebral palsy. From his first year he had a physical therapist, and a team of professionals worked with the family. Though they wanted answers to questions like "Will he ever walk?" "Will he keep up with his peers in school?" the staff at Children's Orthopedic Hospital stressed that trying to answer such questions while David was still so young would only be to his detriment. They told the parents that a rigid diagnosis would only limit David. The staff was concerned about what's been called the self-fulfilling proph- ecy; that once someone is assessed they're treated accordingly by those around them. Even if the person is capable of more, they're often not allowed to try. And so the person begins to mirror the diagnosis, fairly or not.

So instead, Marge concentrated her energies on the parent group that was formed through David's Infant Stimulation class at the Northwest Center. She talked about the federal legislation, Public Law 94-142, that had just been signed that fall. It required appropriate public school education for all handicapped children between the ages of three and twenty-one. "Of course a lot of the specifics have scattered time tables," she added. "Like the certain things that don't have to be put into effect until 1980. But we're lucky with David's being so young. It must have really been hard on your parents."

Marge had had two miscarriages before David was born. And she was concerned when I told her that Betty had had a miscarriage the past year and wanted very much to have a baby.

"Are they worried about having a handicapped child?" she asked.

"I know Philip is," I said.

He had recently told me that Mary Fran completely changed the family. And that he wouldn't be willing to go through that with his child. I had been mad at him for seeing it that way. So simple. Everything neat and easy.

"It certainly does cause extra problems," she admitted. "Not that the problems are even David. I mean, who says that houses should be at the top of a flight of stairs? But just because they are, David's a burden. If buildings had ground level access David wouldn't be a problem. . . . I guess you just start looking at things differently. We can't afford to throw away lives just because they don't fit. I don't know what to make of a society that treasures deviance in buildings and punishes deviance in people. . . . I'm sorry, I don't mean to lecture you."

"You don't have to apologize," I said. "It's a good lecture. I feel like I'm always lecturing my friends. It's nice to be on the listening side for once."

"Well, it helps," she laughed. "It's good to practice on your friends, then you can listen to yourself and try to decide if it's really worth all the fighting."

The next evening when I was at the Radtkes, Mrs. Radtke

asked if I thought Christina would be interested in living with them that summer, to take care of Tom. She had been to the doctor, who had told her that she couldn't go on lifting him in and out of bed, the tub, his wheelchair . . . all the moving and lifting that was part of her day. They planned to make some adaptations in the house that would lessen the lifting. And they had begun to talk about something they had put off for a long time—putting Tom in a residential program. But Mrs. Radtke was much more interested in talking about using funds from the Home Aide Program to hire live-in help. I told her I'd ask Christina. I knew she wanted to stay for the summer. But she didn't want to go to the trouble of finding two roommates to share the rent just for a few months. So she was resigning herself to leaving in June.

I felt much more comfortable with Tom than I had the first time. It was awful to find myself falling into the stereotype behavior of being put off by Tom and charmed by David—what some people call the Poster Child Mentality: they're okay as long as they're young and cute. At first all I saw was what Marge would call "his deviance," just the saliva, and stooped shoulders, and twisted fingers. But the way his mother had talked to him the first day didn't seem as strange as I got to know him.

The next day I asked Christina about Tom. When she asked what he was like I found myself describing him by telling the things we did together, and what his mother was like with him. "Of course, if you asked Barney Weber," I added, "He'd say cerebral palsy, mentally retarded, nonverbal, nonambulatory, not toilet trained . . . " Christina said she'd like to meet Tom and the Radtkes to talk it over.

Of course, all the time we were talking we were accompanied by the sound of the guinea pigs. They seemed to be more noisy than usual.

"I wonder what they're fussing about now," I said.

"I have absolutely no desire to find out," Christina said as she gathered her quilt makings and went upstairs to her bedroom.

I was bending over the cage when Mary Fran came home from the Kiwanis Center. "They're really making a lot of noise tonight," I said to her.

She walked into the living room and leaned over their cage, "What wrong, pigs?" They continued to squeal in a series of short, high pitched phrases that we often imitated to prove to others how unpleasant they were. When they didn't answer her she said, "Silly pigs," and stood up straight. Then she added, "Maybe they going to have babies."

"Wouldn't that be awful!" I said. "No they couldn't, they're all girls."

"Girls have babies," Fran said with a laugh.

"Yeah," I agreed. "But not by themselves."

"Guinea pig not need doctor to help," she said. "They not like people."

"No, that's not what I meant," I said. "I meant in order for a girl to have a baby there has to be a boy around."

"Mo!" Fran said in impatience, "It the girl who have the baby." Then she left the room and walked up to her bedroom.

Oh boy! Fran was taking a bath so I went into Christina's room and repeated our conversation in a whisper.

Christina sat on her bed looking up at me, "So why did you come to me, you want to know which one of you is right?"

"Christina, this isn't funny," I said. "I mean she doesn't even know the basics."

"Then tell her," Christina said simply. "Ah spring . . . "

"Cut it out," I said. "I really don't want to know what Sophocles would say about this. I just want to know what to say."

"Well, why don't you go talk to you-know-who at the Kiwanis Center," she suggested with a broad smile.

"That's a good idea," I said. "Even though you meant it as a lewd suggestion. John Cozzolino probably would be a good person to talk to. Now go back to your quilt. You've been extremely immature about this whole thing, and I hope the pigs get loose and stampede into your bedroom tonight."

Though I was determined to be mature myself I continued to put off going to the Kiwanis Center. One day as I was talking to Mom I asked her if Fran's school had ever offered a sex education course. She said that someone had given a series of classes. But she didn't know what it covered. And she wasn't sure how much of it Fran had understood. I went to the Kiwanis Center that afternoon.

It was aways so comforting to see Molly, the secretary at the front deak. She was always friendly and remembered our names. As she hung up the phone she said, "Maureen, I hope you didn't come to see John. He's not in this afternoon."

"That's alright," I said, feeling great relief. "Would Jane have time to talk to me?"

"Let me look at her schedule," Molly said. "She's pretty busy, but she'll have a little time in about an hour. Do you want to talk to her then?"

"Yes," I said, "That'll be fine."

While I was waiting I walked to the downtown library and went to the children's floor. I looked for sex education books and found some. Then I checked them all out.

Jane listened to me repeat the guinea pig story complete with the squeaking pig imitations. "What do you think?" I asked.

"I think you should get rid of them," she said. "They sound awful."

"Jane!" I said. "Look, I checked out these books. Is this what I should be doing?"

"Okay," she said, "I'll be serious. I think your intention is good. But I really don't think there's anything I can tell you."

"Well, how should I approach it?" I asked. "I mean the old egg and sperm story won't work, will it?"

"There are all sorts of opinions," Jane said. "A lot of people are getting involved now in the whole question of sexual rights of handicapped people. There are books, slide presentations . . . Some people believe you should give specific information at certain ages, and some people believe you don't say anything until asked. Some people even believe you should teach people how to masturbate, and the main concern of others is how to prevent the masturbation that is ocurring. Oh, Maureen, I don't know what to tell you. I wish you'd just take all these books out of here, and go talk to your sister."

At home that afternoon I went through a rehearsal. One of the books I had gotten out of the library was pretty good. And I felt more comfortable with something to hold on to. So I had decided to use it.

That evening I walked into Fran's room and said, "Would you come into my room for a minute, please?" Too stiff, have to loosen up.

"I was just at the library this afternoon . . . " I started as planned and rehearsed, when I noticed the puzzled look on Fran's face. And for a good reason. What *was* I doing? Oh, this is ridiculous, I thought. But I had gone this far, I might as well at least read through the book. We both sat there stiffly on the edge of the bed, trying to predict each other's next move.

After I finished the book I said, "Do you know how babies are made?"

"Like in the book, Mo," she said.

"Can you have a baby?" I asked.

"Not by myself," she giggled. "Have to be girl and boy together."

Why didn't I just ask her that in the first place, I thought. Who cares what she thinks about guinea pigs, they'll be gone in a few days anyway.

"Mo, have to go," Fran said. "Have supper club tonight."

CHAPTER 17

In the spring I continued to see Laura every week or two. We always left the house even if it was just for a walk around the neighborhood. We never had a conversation. I was satisfied if I felt her stiffness easing a little. Sometimes I became frustrated and did little more than put in my time with her.

But early in the year I had decided I should have some idea what was going on, so I had asked Mrs. Barnes if she would mind my calling Laura's doctor. She had agreed. When I had finally gotten in touch with the doctor I made the mistake of referring to Laura as his "patient." He had answered that Laura was his "client," and that she was developing quite well and there was nothing to discuss. I should have known better. In my field many people consider it patronizing to call anyone over sixteen or seventeen a "student," so they all suddenly become "clients."

I had offered asking Mrs. Barnes to send him a note with her signature. No. I could stop by in person. No, there was nothing to talk about. Of course, how silly of me! I was a mere volunteer so what could I know. All her improvements went unnoticed by my untrained eyes. All I knew was that Laura was a teenage girl who suddenly woke up one day completely different–she walked like the Tin Man, didn't talk, and was on some medication but her mother didn't know what for. Laura had dropped her tray the one time we tried to go out to lunch. And there she had stood in the middle of the cafeteria staring down at the broken dishes.

I wish I knew what to do. I kept going back. Not just because I had commited myself. But once in awhile I'd look at her and notice that her eyes didn't seem as glassy. And once when I had given up on her and started talking to myself she had laughed at me. It wasn't her usual hollow laugh, but a real laugh. And I looked at her. She looked back at me. And I felt like saying, "Quick, tell me. What's going on? We're blocks from your house, no one else can hear, just explain it to me." But the shadow had come back and her focus changed as she looked past me as usual.

I called Andrea Wilson, the director of Citizen Advocacy, and reminded her that I'd be leaving in June. I wanted Laura to be put on the list to receive a new advocate. Andrea promised she'd do her best. Though I didn't know what Laura needed, it didn't seem like she could afford to lose anything else; even if that was only a weekly walking partner.

That month there was a craft fair in the university district that was held every April. Mary Fran really wanted to go to it. But I had promised the Thorndikes I'd come in one Saturday to work with David. They wanted to spend the day on a hike with their other two sons. Since David couldn't walk, once he had become too heavy to be carried, they had to give up their weekend hikes.

"We'll have to start early," I told Mary Fran. "Because I have to be at the Thorndikes at two."

"It be easy," she said. "We take number 30 bus and transfer in Ballard."

The bus to the university was the same one that went to Philip and Betty's. She was proud that she knew. I didn't particularly want to spend the morning squeezed between crowds of people and rows of macramed plant hangers. But she didn't give me time to refuse.

When we got to the craft fair the streets that were blocked off were already packed with people. The day was sunny and promised to get even hotter. The stands were set up through the middle of the street and along the sidewalks. One lane of the crowd was going up the street. And the group on the other side was going in the opposite direction. People just drifted into line and then passed by the exhibits at the crowd's pace. Mary Fran led us into line and appreciatively eyed the booths. I followed trying to see through the crowd and figure out how much further we had to go.

Mary Fran maneuvered her way through the crowds to get to a display of embroidered shirts. She liked to do needlework, and enjoyed seeing the things other people did. I followed slowly, moving with the flow of the crowd. Soon everything began to blur into a mass of candles, painted driftwood, and macrame. The sun was getting hotter. Someone ahead of me decided to stop. And I obediently stopped when I saw a man's back an inch from my eyes. Looking to the left I saw a display of crewel.

"Fran, did you see this?" I asked pointing to the crewel.

But she was nowhere around. Tapping on the man's back I squeezed past a few bodies thinking that she was ahead of me. Eventually I made my way out of the crowd in the street, and up to the curb where there was more room. What did she have on today? I tried to remember. Jeans and her red T-shirt. No, the T-shirt was dirty. She had on her blue striped blouse. That's right, she put that blouse on this morning.

Everyone seemed to be wearing blue shirts. I walked down the sidewalk trying to be calm as my eyes frantically scanned the crowd. Ten blocks later I came to the end of the booths. Three policemen talked and laughed as they leaned against the barricades that closed off the street. I wanted to ask them for help. But I felt like I would be betraying her in front of strangers. I imagined them asking, "Your sister's twenty-three and she's lost?"

"Well, she's mentally retarded."

"Uh-oh, we got a retardate lost somewhere in the university district."

So I walked on. I retraced my route going back on the other side of the street. Moving quickly I scanned the crowd . . . blue striped blouse . . . blue striped blouse. I looked down at my watch and saw that I had only forty minutes before I had to be at work. A headache pounded away behind my eyes. I kept looking, scanning the crowd, trying to see through the people.

Okay, this is ridiculous, I told myself. Just calm down. First, find a phone and call the Thorndikes. Explain that you'll be late. Then just keep looking, you'll find her eventually. But I refused to take my own advice. They'd have to cancel their hiking trip. If I could just concentrate, I thought, I'll be able to find her.

I began to suspect that I had died and gone to hell. If hell is personalized this would be a perfect one for me: being stuck in the middle of a mob of strangers where I was forced to look at table after table of scented candles. An added twist would be that I repeatedly had to force my way between the people and booths in search of Mary Fran who I had let down by allowing us to be separated.

This must be a fantastic growing experience, I thought, because it sure is awful. At least I could appease myself with the thought that it was character building. I was almost back at the beginning of the fair by the crewel. There's another damned blue striped shirt, I thought, as my eyes quickly passed by. But I looked back in time to see that this one really was Mary Fran's. She stood quietly, one hand nervously tearing at a finger nail. She was by the booth with the embroidered shirts.

"Fran, where have you been?" I asked. "I've been looking all over for you."

"Here," she answered. "Couldn't see you, so waited for you here."

"Well, I'm glad you stayed in one place," I said as I touched her shoulder to reassure myself that I had found her. "We're going to have to leave," I added. "I have to get to work."

"Too bad," she said as she followed me to the bus stop. "It a nice fair."

"You didn't miss much," I told her. "I ran through it a couple of times. It's almost all candles up there."

When I got to the Thorndikes my headache was still hanging on. I looked at my watch and saw that I was fifteen minutes late. So far not a very promising day, I thought, as I ran up the steps that led to their front lawn. Mrs. Thorndike had told me they would probably have to move soon since David was getting too heavy to carry up and down the steps everyday. I expected David's two brothers, Todd and Rob, to be sitting impatiently on the lawn. But the front door was open and everyone was sitting on the living room floor, laughing and talking excitedly.

David's mother, Marge, looked up from the floor where everyone was kneeling around David. "We're celebrating," she explained.

"I knew he could do it," David's father said as he beamed in delight.

" 'reen!" David called out to welcome me. He was holding on to the couch as he stood with his casts on his legs. They were put on twice a day to help develop his muscles, as well as to prevent a spinal curvature from developing.

"He took his first steps," Marge explained. "He had his casts on and I was walking him, I never expected it to happen. I was holding him by his shoulders but I really wasn't paying attention. I was trying to remember if I had everything packed in the car. . . ."

". . . And he walked without crossing his feet in front of each other," Rob added excitedly.

"It's called 'scissoring,' " Todd corrected. Then he added, looking at me, "He didn't scissor."

"I know what it's called," Rob insisted. "But I wasn't sure if Maureen knew."

"You're lying," Todd said. "You didn't say it 'cause you didn't know. Maureen's a teacher, she knows that stuff."

"She's not a real teacher," Rob said. "She's not finished with college yet."

"Okay, boys," their father interrupted. "That's enough. Let's see if we have everything in the car. We have to leave soon."

After they left the room Marge placed David on his back and started taking the casts off. "I think that's enough for the casts today," she said as she knelt over him. "Don't you, Davey?"

"Yeah," he agreed as his face broke into a dimpled grin. " 'Enough for today!' 'reen here, play bus stop now!"

"You want to play bus stop with her, huh?" she said with a laugh as she pulled on the velcro that held the two plaster halves of the cast together. She wrapped them together with quick, sure movements as her eyes looked out the large picture window and followed Rob, who ran down the steps to the car carrying a thermos. Then she put the casts in their regular place next to the couch.

"This is what Jerry's been waiting for," she said to me as she named her husband. "Whenever I bring up the idea of selling the house and moving to a place with ground level access he gets furious. He thinks it would be a sign of giving up on David ever walking. I think he still expects David to be able to join the soccer team he coaches. Of course, next year when Davey goes to the public school's pre-school program he'll be in a wheelchair. Seeing him that way will make it seem so much more definite. But the only thing we can do is wait and see how he developes."

"What about this summer?" I asked. "Will David be in school?"

"We just went to a meeting about that last night," she said, her face showing exasperation. Then she explained the problems the parents had discussed—funding, staff, and transportation. "I think we'll be able to work it out, it isn't even May yet. But what Jerry and I are most concerned about," she added, "Is where David will go in the fall. There are about three schools he could go to. Now that the federal law about mandatory special ed. has passed we could do what they call 'contract out.' "

"Is that where you can pick your child's school?" I asked.

"That's sort of what it means," she answered. "It was started because they realized that making it a law that handicppaed children were eligible to attend public schools wouldn't be any good in areas where the public school system didn't have a special ed. program. So, in those cases the parent can send their child to a private special ed. school and the public school system pays for it. It makes sense because we're taxpayers, too," she added defensively.

"You don't have to convince me," I said. "I think it's about time."

"The sticky part comes when the public school system has a special ed. program," she said, "But not one that fits the needs of your child. So you still want to 'contract out' to a private special ed. school."

"Are you going to have problems?" I asked.

"I don't think so," she said. "Some of the staff at Children's Orthopedic Hospital have written evaluations that back up our opinion about . . . "

"Mom, come on!" Rob interrupted as he stood panting for breath outside the screen door.

"I'm coming," she answered. "Is everyone in the car?"

"We've been ready forever!" he said melodramatically.

"Robert, don't be a smarty!" she said sharply as she left the living room and started up the stairs.

Todd came running up to join Rob on the front porch. "Where's Mom?" he asked as he squinted through the screen door.

"She went upstairs to get something," Rob answered.

"Robbbbert!" David called as he crawled out from under the dining room table where he had been playing with a toy.

"Oh, no!" Todd said. "Now he's going to start crying when he sees us leaving."

"No he won't," Rob answered. "Davey, Davey Crockett," he sang as his brother crawled across the floor to the door. David laughed in delight. Rob opened the screen door and went inside to where his brother lay on the floor. He picked up his feet and swung his legs. Then he started to sing, "David Ravid Bo Bavid, Banana Fana Fo Favid, Fee Fi Mo Mavid, Daavid!"

"Okay, is everyone ready?" Marge asked as she came rushing down the stairs and into the living room. She bent over David as she passed by, "Give me a kiss. We'll see you tonight, Davey, have fun." Then she directed Todd and Rob to the door, "Let's get going, boys, before your father gives up on us."

A few weeks later I got a call from my boss, Barney Weber. I seldom saw him since I went directly to the families' houses. And on paydays the checks were mailed to me. He started the conversation in his usual way: with a question.

"What do you know about epilepsy, Maureen?" he asked.

"A little bit," I answered. "I've worked at camps where a few of the kids were epileptic. And my sister had petit mal seizures because of her brain damage when she was little."

"That's good enough for me," he answered. "I have a request for respite care. The client is two years old. She has grand mal seizures. Are you interested?"

"Respite care," I repeated. "So I'd just take the 'client' to the park? That kind of thing?"

"Excellent idea, Maureen!" he said, as if it were truly the most innovative idea he had heard all day. Maybe it was. "Let me see what else it says here. . . . The mother made a request for a two-week period. It seems she's in the process of moving and is busy with her infant, her little girl, and five teenage foster children. To be quite frank, Maureen, we're not clear on the eligibility of the case. We are, after all, the Bureau of Developmental Disabilities. If the client has brain damage as a result of the seizures she would clearly be termed developmentally disabled. But if it is solely epilepsy . . . well, we're not sure. But this time we're letting it through."

Winkie turned out to be a darling little girl with curly black hair and big brown eyes. She still wasn't talking much, but she was gregarious in her own way. I just hoped she'd keep smiling and humming. She seemed so tiny to have grand mal seizures.

I couldn't remember Mary Fran's seizures. But when I was sixteen, and working at a camp, one of my campers had a seizure. The first time it happened the other counselors were calm and organized about it. But I hadn't been able to do anything but stand and stare. Everyone commented later on how suprised they were at my reaction. I was surprised too. Later I found out from Mom about Fran's seizures. But I do remember the EEG, brain wave scan, that must have been done after one of the seizures. I remember it because of the friendly woman in the white coat who took the time to explain to me why she had to put the sticky stuff on my sister's hair and what the wires were for.

I also remember it because Mary Fran and I spent many weeks afterward giving EEG's to our dolls. We'd sit down in the basement where we'd make a sticky paste out of detergent and water. We'd spread it in the doll's hair. Tide detergent became our electrode paste. Then the ribbons and bobby pins became an elaborate network of machines and wires. We assured our dolls that everything was fine, it wasn't going to hurt a bit, it was just a simple test. Eventually we began to believe out own words, and got bored with that game and went on to something else.

Winkie liked to play with dolls. But more than that she liked to walk. She had just begun to walk a few months earlier and her pudgy little legs carried her forward in an unsteady, excited gait. It was the beginning of May and getting very sunny. So every morning Winkie and I would start out for our walk to the park. Sometimes we had to share the park with rambunctious big kids from the neighborhood elementary school. But usually there were just a few mothers with their young children who were close to Winkie's age.

One day when we got to the park it was completely empty.

Winkie took off for the slide where she started to climb the ladder. As soon as she sat down on the top I ran around to the bottom to catch her. Her coordination wasn't developed enough for her to be able to land on her feet. So I always caught her at the botom and helped her stand.

On about the third trip when I was running from the ladder back to the slide, I saw a Volvo station wagon pull up to the curb. A mother and a young girl about Winkie's age got out. The woman seemed relieved to see someone else at the park. She came up to the slide and gave me a smiling welcome of the kind I had seen the mothers exchange.

"Another beautiful day at the park," she said to me.

"It is nice to have the sun out," I said before I realized that she was being facetious.

She settled cross-legged on the ground as she sighed, "It's just so mindless."

She reminded me of some of the people I had met at universities. Intense hooded eyes staring out of a flat, static face. And always, that low drawn-out voice that seemed determined to make even a shopping list sound profound.

Her eyes settled on Winkie as she asked, "How old is your daughter?"

"Two," I answered. I decided it was none of her business that Winkie had epilepsy. And that would come out if I said she wasn't my daughter.

"It *is* difficult not to be too protective, isn't it?" she said with a combination of amusement and disapproval as she watched me race between the ladder and the end of the slide.

I was too busy being overprotective to answer.

"Her gait is quite unsteady," she said. "Has she reached her developmental milestones in appropriate time?"

"She has been a bit slow," I answered tersely. I couldn't believe this was happening. It was like a cartoon, competitive mothers thrashing it out at the park.

"If I were you I'd have a complete work-up done on her," she advised. "The University of Washington Hospital is a wonderful facility. Now our Stephanie . . . "

"Look," I said sharply, "She has epilepsy. Now I don't know if you really know what you're talking about or not. But with her frequent severe seizures, and having to adjust to anti-convulsant medication, I don't feel like putzing around talking about 'milestones.' The way she's compensating is tremendous. You are looking at one brilliant kid! And I don't mean little Stephanie."

I guess I originally hoped to shock her into silence. But once I got going I got sort of carried away. But she didn't seem at all affected. It's amazing how difficult it is to offend some people.

"Epilepsy, yes," she said slowly as if she were mentally flipping through a file. "It's too bad; the thing to remember is to carefully monitor her seizures. Of course, having epilepsy doesn't mean your daughter can't live a normal life."

And with that gem of wisdom we settled into a truce of silence.

CHAPTER 18

Betty had recently had her car fixed and she loaned it to me our last week as we rushed around getting ready to leave. I was still working at the Thorndikes and Radtkes. And Mary Fran was still working at the Northwest Center and going to the Kiwanis Center at night. It seemed hard to believe that in less than a week we'd both be back in Michigan. I had never stayed away from home for so long before. And Fran . . . we had no idea what she'd go back to.

On my way back from the Thorndikes I sat behind a row of cars waiting for the bridge to go back down. I looked over at the photo album on the car seat. The Thorndikes had given it to me as a going away present. Todd and Rob had signed their names inside the cover, and David drew on it with a felt pen. When I got back I'd have to stay around the house in case anyone else answered our ad. We were trying to sell the few pieces of furniture that we had accumulated over the year. While I was home I could call the phone and gas companies. Then the next day I had to be at the Radtkes.

And our last day before going to the airport, we were going out to lunch with Philip and Betty.

When I got to the Radtkes the next day, Mrs. Radtke was busy packing. They were leaving for a family reunion in South Dakota. She was well-organized as usual. But bustling around refolding clothes and moving suitcases helped to keep her mind off the fact that they were going to be leaving Tom for two weeks. He's eighteen, I thought to myself in amazement, and this is the first time they've ever gone anywhere without him.

"Oh, Maureen," she said as she came out of one of the bedrooms. "I'm so glad Christina has agreed to live-in this summer. Now are you sure we didn't push her into it? Are you sure she really wants to?"

"Yes," I assured her. "She's glad to have the chance to stay here for a few extra months. I think it will work out great for everyone. And try to relax. Christina's a regular girl scout—strong, dependable, and trustworthy."

"It's not that I don't trust her," she said with a strained smile. "I'm just edgy . . . Ever since we started talking about putting Tom in the Cerebral Palsy Residential Center, the kids have suddenly started talking about their childhood. The other day Mariann came over to tell me that I never loved her, that Tom got all the attention. Do you say things like that to your mother?"

"I suppose I have," I answered. "No, I'm not sure . . . Once in a while, but I guess I don't say much because I'm not sure how I feel. But I've been keeping a journal . . . "

"And someday you'll probably turn it into a book," she said teasingly. "You kids either slap us in our face with your words, or you write about it for everyone to read."

As we stood facing each other our smiles faded and some of the pain oozed out. She was no longer the employer and I, the tutor. We were simply a mother and a daughter as we strained to explain ourselves to our invisible families.

"It wasn't easy," I said. "We always played together, we were best friends. But I still knew that if it came down to the two of us she'd always win. It was always her they'd go to first. I remember watching her and wanting so badly to get some of the attention she got."

"She got enough attention," Mrs. Radtke answered. "I didn't have much time, but I certainly never ignored her. . . . At least I never meant to. It's just that he needed me so much."

The next day, Saturday, we finally seemed to have everything packed just as Betty and Philip drove up. Christina would be moving to the Radtkes that night. After we got our suitcases into the trunk, the five of us headed for a restaurant that Philip insisted everyone had to eat in at least once. All he told us was that it was a Chinese restaurant in the International District. When we asked him more about it, he said enthusiastically, "It'll be real crowded because it's lunch time."

"Oh, Phil, maybe we should go someplace else," Betty suggested. "The girls might miss their plane."

Philip checked the rear view mirror as he moved into the left lane. "No, no, it'll be fine. . . . You're going to love it."

When we got there we climbed the two flights up to the restaurant and realized immediately that Philip had been right . . . it really was crowded. Once we were seated Philip said, "This is not your typical Chinese-food-for-Americans restaurant." He explained that you had to ask the waiters for dishes from their trays as they passed between the tables. Christina watched us joke as we pointed out our choices and said, "You guys act like you never get out!"

"Our mother used to always say that," Philip said in surprise. "Oh, Mo told you that . . . here Mo, try this."

"Everybody's mother told them that," I said taking the dish he passed to me. "Well, almost everyone's mother," I added smiling over at Betty.

Most of the food was cooked Szechuan style so it was hot and spicy. But the dishes were new to all of us, except Betty who had been there with Philip before. Philip's enthusiasm was just like a little boy's wanting to show off a wonderful new discovery.

As I bit into the last dish he had put in front of me I felt like I was chewing on a marshmallow in hot sauce. "What is it?" I asked.

"Which one are you eating?" Betty asked. When I pointed to the dish she said, "I don't think you want to know."

"Betty, don't be gross," Philip said using the admonishment she always used on us. "It's tripe, my dear."

"Oh," I said, deciding that I really didn't like tripe. Then I realized that I didn't know what tripe was. "What's that?"

Betty's face broke into a look of pure delight as she pronounced clearly, "The lining of the stomach of cattle."

"Betty!" Fran said in disgust.

I stopped smiling and very quickly stopped chewing. "Philip?" I asked.

"Sometimes from sheep or goats," he said. "But usually it is from a cow."

Soon after that we left for the airport. And there it finally hit us—our year was up. As it turned out many more things were discovered and shared than even the most optimistic in our family had hoped.

Our confidence in Mary Fran was proven not to be just "a biased family's pathetic hope" as many professionals had insinuated through the years. But we fought the desire to see this as a happy ending. The past twenty years had taught us that there would be many more ups and downs in trying to prove that these new accomplishments of Mary Fran's represented her capability to go even further.

During the year I was able to see myself as my sister saw me. She opened herself to me in her times of hopelessness. The only thing she asked was that she be taken seriously and not nervously wiped aside with glib jokes or optimistic predictions.

She didn't trust my optimism. She didn't think it could be true for her. Because from Mary Fran's viewpoint, I am a winner. To her it seems that things come easily to me—words

– 161 –

flow, colleges accept, friends gather. I tried to tell her it wasn't true. I wanted us to be the equals that we were when we were little—before Our Lady of Providence, before St. John's, before Arlington Workshop, before Carleton College.

It was so much easier when we were young enough to believe our parents. They had told us, "Being mentally retarded just means that sometimes you're slower in some things, that's all. People understand that." I think they knew it wasn't true. It wasn't true for them. But maybe they hoped that if they said it often enough it would become true for us.

Mary Fran began to see that things didn't always come easily to me. But she is probably right about me in a lot of ways. I'll finish college. Then I'll probably go to graduate school and fulfill my little-girl dream of being the psychologist my parents would have liked.

But the thing Mary Fran doesn't know is that I'm still very much her younger sister. Though I may eventually have a series of degrees after my name, and my terminololgy may become more clinical, it is those early years that have had the most influence on me. My sister, who has come to think of most learning situations as causing little but failure and embarrassment, has been my most important teacher.

But what about her? What she will become, I don't know. I sometimes imagine us in twenty or thirty years. In my imagination we live near each other and get together to talk or do errands or share dinner. We're not that different from the way we are now. But I know things will change. She is changing now. She used to be satisfied to get along on her smile. In our family she was always The Loving One, just as Patricia was The Talented One. But Mary Fran decided that wasn't enough. And it was her anger that carried her into a whole new world.

I wonder what will happen if, in the future, she ever needs me again as much as she did the fall we went to Seattle. I don't know if I will always be willing to go on being the Earth Mother, The Responsible One. I don't think I want to, not always. But I'm not sure that has much to do with it. It's not as easy as saying, "I'd prefer not to."

Maybe when we're old we'll live together again. Maybe we'll grow senile together, trying to pick the burrs out of the smooth cloth of our memories. Leaning close to my hearing aid she'll shout, "I can't do it!" "I don't have a nickel and a quarter!" "Don't leave me!" And she'll wobble to the front door feeling like her seven-year-old self dropped off at Our Lady of Providence. And I'll scream after her, "Are they taking you to the doctor's again? Can I go too?" "Do you know which bus to take?" "Did you hate me?" I'll want to ask, "Did you hate me for outgrowing you?" What crazy old ladies we'd be. Handing out zucchini bread to the neighborhood kids in the daylight and screaming out our hurt in the evening's darkness.

Our plane was circling the airport. We'd be landing soon. We sat next to each other in silence, both busy with our own thoughts.

Before leaving Seattle we were cleaning up in the kitchen and we had time to reminisce about the friends who had visited and the special meals we had all cooked together. Mary Fran had said that she'd like to have her own apartment in three years, she thought she'd be ready by then. I asked her what kind of apartment she wanted and she had answered—something near a bus line, where she could have a cat of her own, and a bottle of wine on the shelf for when friends dropped by.

EPILOGUE

In August of 1978, two years after Mary Fran and I had left Seattle, we went back again. Philip and Betty met us at the airport as they had the first time. But this time it was raining.

The past two years had included so much. When we left in 1976, we both felt so proud of our accomplishments that we wouldn't have been at all surprised if a marching band and a crowd with banners had greeted us at the small Benton Harbor airport.

Mom was there. And during the thirty-minute ride home, she assured us that she had been talking to some people in a nearby city. There were a few sheltered workshops and vocational training programs. But the thing she was most excited about was that there seemed to be a good chance that Mary Fran could move into a semi-independent apartment program that was just starting. Mary Fran was pleased that she'd be able to continue her independence and still have the security of Mom's being nearby in South Haven.

But something happened once Mary Fran arrived. Suddenly the social workers and program directors were busy with meetings. When they did have a few minutes off the phone or out of the conference rooms, they reminded Mom that the plans they had spoken about were "pending," just maybes. But my mother had become a businesswoman after Dad's death. And she's a very capable and astute one. I hate the hysterical parent thesis. And I know it just doesn't apply here. My mother can certainly tell the difference between a program that's presented as pending and one that is said to be opening any day.

I think I know what happened. Because I have a foot in both worlds, I'm often in the clumsy situation of seeing both sides–the professionals' and the family members'. It probably seems strange to someone not involved to think of there being sides. It seems ridiculous to most of us. Many times I don't want anything to do with either side; not the single-mindedness and intense emotions of the family members or the pragmatic actions and jargon-filled rhetoric of the professionals. But wanted or not, I've got it.

One thing common to all professionals in my field is the dark little corner in them yearning to be a savior. Maybe it's because they–I really have to say we–work in a field where there is such intense need for a savior. Even a couple of saviors. They could be spread out by regions to ease the load, the Eastern Seaboard Savior, the Midwest Savior, and so on. Since there would only be a limited number of savior positions available, the rest of us would have to settle for having a school or group home named after us. I don't mean to go too far. Because the truth is we've all seen the incredible jumps that students can make when paired with a teacher who somehow manages to make a connection in a way no one else ever has. It has the thrill of a sort of miracle. And we've felt the intense pleasure of being part of that. And the delight when someone comments on the student's change. On our best days we don't need the compliments. They're nice to hear, but they aren't what keep us going. And on our worst days, we're sure that it would have happened anyway, even if we weren't there.

No matter how much in control you think you have your savior fantasy, it would be too much to resist this concerned mother with a story of twenty-three years of ups and downs and then the dramatic year in Seattle. But the problem is, it's one thing to spend an hour or so with the personable mother. You make a few idealistic comments about possible upcoming plans and then sit back and bask in her gratitude. And it's a whole other thing when the daughter arrives on the scene. This must be what happened. I've heard other family members tell of similar experiences. And during our year in Seattle, I had a very similar thing happen to me at one of the agencies I went to. But I also know that as our search continued I became more desperate, and started grasping at maybes like they were signed affidavits. So here we are, back in the middle again looking at both sides.

Though the apartment training program didn't exist, Mary Fran didn't live at home. One of the social workers told Mom that there was an opening in a group home for six women. Though the others were much older than Fran, in their forties and fifties, the social worker said it would be a good place while she waited. So that summer she moved into the group home and worked at a sheltered workshop. There was concern among the staff in her workshop—just where had this new client been during 1976? So the social worker called Mom asking for evaluations. Mom repeated her description of the year. "There wasn't really any one single program," she tried to explain. "Well, just send me whatever you can," the social worker replied.

Knowing that it would be to Fran's detriment not to have anything, we started with the reference from the rest home where she had volunteered. A letter to the Kiwanis Center resulted in an evaluation from the speech therapist. Though I wrote Sheila, called her twice, and she promised to send an evaluation, she never did. Okay, I thought, if they want an evaluation, I'll write them an evaluation. That night I typed up the three pages that I had written. And the next day I left for New York. I got there in time to register for the summer session. Then I moved in with my sister, Patricia, and her roommates, where I lived for the summer before moving into my own apartment in the fall.

The next year went very fast for both of us. I finished college and got a job working in a group home. And Mary Fran was transferred from the sheltered workshop to a day program that was better for her. It was a vocational training program with classes in the morning and piece work in the workshop in the afternoon.

The following year the main concern for both of us was group homes. Mary Fran was still living in the same one, even though a year-and-a-half had passed. She spent every other weekend home with Mom. There she often complained about the other women babying her. "They don't know how much me do in Seattle," she would say. She would talk about being repeatedly reminded about her chores instead of being left to remember them on her own. And she told Mom she looked forward to moving out, when she would no longer always have "someone on my tail."

Though I was in no mood to hear Mom's stories about staff incompetence, I sometimes turned the tables on her and complained about parents. Occasionally I talked with Fran. But she had never become that comfortable talking on the phone unless she had a definite request or comment to make. And the tension among the frequently bickering women in her group didn't make her any more relaxed.

That summer Mary Fran decided to try to learn how to read. While she was on vacation from her day program she moved out of the group home and back with Mom. Mom agreed to drive her to reading lessons that lasted for an hour every morning. And I quit my job in the group home and planned to start graduate school in the fall.

In the meantime Mom had heard from a man in Chicago who was interested in buying our house for a weekend home. It looked like the negotiations would soon be coming to a close. And Mom was surprised that even though there had been so many false starts she was still sad to have finally found a buyer.

Besides Mary Fran's daily lessons, she took cards and work sheets home and drilled herself every night. When she started the lessons she knew the alphabet and could print her name. Her tutor let her know that she had no question that Fran was capable. She continued to work at home. Sometimes she became frustrated by the babyish level of material she had to work on. But by the end of the eight weeks she had learned the sounds for all the letters, one key word for each letter, could write her name and the alphabet, and could easily read a beginning SRA reader.

Though Mary Fran's tutor had most of her experience working with learning disabled students, she didn't concern herself with whether Fran should be classified as brain damaged or mentally retarded. But she did find it incredible that no one had ever tried to work with her on reading. She said she couldn't understand why "such training wasn't given to Mary in the schools she's attended. Twenty-five years is a long time to wait to learn to read when the potential is there and the interest is high." But she stressed that it was much more than learning an academic skill. "The change in Mary's personality when she not only improved her self-image but also practiced the abstract thinking demanded by reading, writing, and spelling was profound."

So with a summer of hard work behind her, we decided to go to Seattle for a visit. It was a very different trip than the last time. For one thing, we had a fifteen-month-old nephew to get acquainted with. Both of his grandfathers had been named George. So Betty and Philip decided there was little choice, George it would be.

Mary Fran had the presents for George, and I had my camera and enough film to illustrate a dozen issues of *National Geographic*. "Don't care what Mom says," Mary Fran said, "Gonna give him a lot of presents. Me his aunt, that what I supposed to do—spoil him!" And for once I agreed completely.

I could see that it was raining in Seattle. But I didn't care. It was so wonderful to come with nothing to prove, no battles to fight. We were just visitors who had once lived there, and were now coming in from out of town. We were two doting aunts bustling through the connecting ramp, itching to get our hands on our unsuspecting nephew.

The Edge of Terror

*The Heroic Story of American Families
Trapped in the Japanese-occupied
Philippines*

Scott Walker

Thomas Dunne Books
St. Martin's Press ⚜ New York

THOMAS DUNNE BOOKS.
An imprint of St. Martin's Press.

THE EDGE OF TERROR. Copyright © 2009 by Scott Walker. All rights reserved. Printed in the United States of America. For information, address St. Martin's Press, 175 Fifth Avenue, New York, N.Y. 10010.

www.thomasdunnebooks.com
www.stmartins.com

Maps by Donald S. Frazier, Ph.D.
Book design by Omar Chapa

Library of Congress Cataloging-in-Publication Data

Walker, Scott, 1950–
    The edge of terror: the heroic story of American families trapped in the Japanese-occupied Philippines / Scott Walker. — 1st ed.
        p. cm.
    Includes bibliographical references and index.
    ISBN 978-0-312-33834-3
    1. Philippines—History—Japanese occupation, 1942–1945.
2. World War, 1939–1945—Philippines.   3. Americans—
Philippines—History—20th century.   4. Baptists—Philippines—
History—20th century.   5. Missionaries—Philippines—History—20th
century.   I. Title.
    DS686.4.W35 2009
    940.53'16108130599–dc22

                                                            2009017341

First Edition: October 2009

10   9   8   7   6   5   4   3   2   1